The Future of Whole Language

Reconstruction or Self-destruction?

Susan M. Church

Heinemann
Portsmouth, NH

Heinemann
A subsidiary of Reed Elsevier, Inc.
361 Hanover Street
Portsmouth, NH 03801-3912
Offices and agents throughout the world

Acquisitions Editor: Toby Gordon
Production and Copy Editor: Renée M. Nicholls
Cover Designer: Barbara Werden

Library of Congress Cataloging-in-Publication Data
Susan M. Church.
   The future of whole language : reconstruction or self-destruction? /
Susan M. Church.
     p.   cm.
   Includes bibliographical references and index.
   ISBN 0-435-08882-3
   1. Language experience approach in education.   2. Politics and
education.   I. Title.
   LB1576.C5567   1996
   372'.6'044—dc20   95-51253
                                                                            CIP

Printed in the United States of America on acid-free paper
99 98 97 96   DA   1 2 3 4 5

To Don,
tap dancer, juggler, gourmet cook,
and husband extraordinaire.

Contents

Foreword

*A*s you'll discover in *The Future of Whole Language: Reconstruction or Self-destruction?*, Susan Church and I have been colleagues and friends for more than fifteen years. The important thing about our collaboration is that from the outset it has never been one-sided. I may have been "the teacher" when we met, but ever since that day, Susan has been asking questions that have pushed me to consider my assumptions and values about literacy learning and about teaching. From the very beginning I have learned as much as, if not more than, Susan has learned from me. In 1980, when Susan joined my teacher study group, her contributions as a resource teacher made the rest of us realize that there were many more questions we needed to be asking ourselves. Working together, we struggled to develop a classroom practice that utilized what the *new* research was telling us about children's spoken and written language development.

In those days, what has come to be called *constructivist* theories of learning were just being fleshed out. Kenneth Goodman's miscue research had recently shown how readers of all ages used a combination of pragmatic, semantic, syntactic, as well as graphophonic cues to make sense of print. Frank Smith's ground-breaking comprehensive synopsis of reading research made a strong case for reading being only incidentally visual. These psycholinguists were making it very clear that reading was considerably more complex than merely transcribing print to sound. We now understood that meaning was at the heart of any literacy activity—that readers needed to bring more to the page than they received from the print.

A component of our class work involved working with at-risk children in a "clinic" setting. We were exploring how to implement literacy instruction that was more comprehensive than the phonics-based, workbook-controlled reading programs prevalent at that time. We were attempting to find ways of building on students' strengths.

Up until that point, remedial reading instruction had been operating from a medical model—find the "disease" and offer a "cure." A psycholinguistic analysis offered an alternative: examine children's strategies, support those that are functional, and provide experiences that permit children to experiment with new strategies. Instead of trying to "fix" kids, we were trying to learn ways of following their lead.

The teachers and I were working to build instructional contexts, which we would subsequently call *whole language*, that focused on meaning and helping students become strategic about reading. We also believed writing to be an essential part of literacy instruction; we were experimenting with a variety of writing activities as part of our reading instruction.

Our particular interest, then, was in developing literacy instruction that would allow students at risk, students from low income backgrounds, and students with learning difficulties to discover how to make sense of written language. While we were interested in literacy instruction generally, we were particularly concerned about helping children who were already, or were in danger of becoming, nonreaders.

As Susan notes, our efforts to change our instructional practices led to resistance from other teachers and administrators. By challenging the prevailing views about literacy instruction, the teachers and I were placing ourselves outside of the mainstream. We were so intent on discovering ways of inviting students into literacy that we really didn't consider the political ramifications of our work. And, although we had a tacit understanding of the political dimension of what we were doing, we didn't recognize the importance of articulating our political agenda and making it explicit.

Over the next several years, Susan and I, as members of a growing collective of Nova Scotia teachers, worked to develop and implement literacy instruction based on a different but solid theoretical framework. Some of the underlying assumptions included:

- knowledge is dynamic;
- learning is social and a natural consequence of performance;
- learning/teaching is a negotiated construction of meaning;
- problem solving is an inherent aspect of literacy development;
- writing and reading are inextricably linked.

We wrote about our work; we gave workshops; we taught courses. Susan played a key role in the development of a new provincial language arts guidelines document, and she and I worked closely with Patricia Barnes, the language arts consultant, to develop teacher networks and to plan the next province-wide curriculum implementation steps.

However, something unexpected happened. With the adoption of the new provincial guidelines came an expectation and a need for teacher inservice. Up to that point, teachers had been exploring literacy largely voluntarily. Now literacy inservices were being mandated. As Susan describes in several places in *The Future of Whole Language: Reconstruction or Self-destruction?*, those of us involved in inservice efforts were being placed in a position that violated one of our fundamental beliefs: learning/teaching is a negotiated construction of meaning.

Many inservice sessions consisted largely in the transmission of information—there was neither the time nor the funds to do much more. Although we attempted to engage groups of teachers in reading and writing experiences, there was no way for people to assimilate the complex ideas and arguments underpinning a whole language theoretical framework. Our best efforts were reduced by the teachers to "nifty tips."

In fact, these inservices likely did more harm than good because they polarized teachers—there were those who attempted to buy into the new instruction and those who felt they were being blamed for students' literacy deficiencies. A good deal of resentment was generated. Although many teachers did go along with the various inservice efforts and complied by incorporating some of the recommended instruction activities into their teaching, there were few supports to permit them to integrate the theoretical framework—to make it their own. Consequently, classroom literacy instruction changed relatively little. Aside from superficial changes, the complex orchestration of cueing systems and strategies required for proficient reading and writing were never fully understood or appreciated by the majority of teachers who came to call themselves *whole language* teachers.

As someone who has grown with and through *whole language*, Susan describes her building sense of frustration as the whole language *movement* began developing. She recounts how she watched as whole language grew "from a loosely coupled network of small groups of teachers and teacher-educators scattered across North America to a full-scale, sometimes disturbingly messianic, worldwide movement" (xx). She notes how as "more and more individual teachers (and sometimes whole districts), embraced whole language it became increasingly ill-defined and diverse" (xx).

As Susan points out, the problem that occurred when whole language ideas began to spread was that a host of orthodoxies was spawned, leaving teachers with a very limited understanding of the complex issues integral to this theoretical framework. Even more serious was the fact that with the spread of the movement, the social issues were lost. When textbook publishers entered the arena, the materials offered to students and teachers became homogenized and concern for students in trouble dissipated. A spirit of inquiry turned into instructional certainty; "it depends" became "you should." Instead of instruction being contextually bound, prescriptions (this time whole language prescriptions) became the norm.

As well, the spread of whole language occurred at a time when the economy was beginning to be forced to downsize and the country took on more and more conservative political values. A literacy perspective that argued for inclusive education, for providing engaging opportunities for all students, for learning as a collaborative endeavor, flew in the face of the political shift to the right. The championing of alternative forms of assessment; of creating inviting learning environments for special needs, ethnically diverse, economically disadvantaged students; of teacher as well as student empowerment, was perceived by business, by government, by parents to be too radical. Whole language became an easy target for anyone wanting tighter control of schools.

The attacks began with pronouncements of a decline in standards—in literacy standards. Much of the fuss had to do with spelling and the apparent absence of explicit phonics instruction in the curriculum.

The financial and other resource cutbacks also began taking their toll. Class sizes began increasing. Money for diverse instructional materials began disappearing. Currently, separate consortia of both the western provinces and the Atlantic provinces have developed learning outcomes and standards documents for several curricular areas, language arts being prominent among them. While the content of these new curriculum policy papers is up-to-date, the tone is clearly one of regulation and control—these are the desired outcomes, and here's how we're going to make certain you're teaching to achieve them. There's no recognition of the enormous diversity within the student population; that increasing numbers of students have severe problems both in school and in their lives; that in the new, large, amalgamated school divisions supports for classroom teachers have largely been eroded; and that student growth is contextually bound. These new policy documents would have us believe that schooling and curriculum preparation are apolitical.

In *The Future of Whole Language: Reconstruction or Self-destruction?* Susan Church details her personal experiences as a whole language teacher and administrator. She shares with us her beginnings as an educator and takes us through her growing understanding of the need for a political analysis of schooling. She recounts critical incidents that helped her understand the tensions of teaching and the political realities of schools. She shows how she came to realize that silence and compliance have political consequences and how this understanding has affected her work with teachers.

Through critical incidents, both personal and of other teachers/educators, Susan makes it clear that the world of school, of classrooms, is a political arena. In today's climate of shrinking resources, the competition among social groups for their share of those limited resources is becoming fierce. Yet, she makes a strong case for reinventing whole language—for not abandoning the fundamental values of this theoretical perspective. She argues that whole language, in a more politically aware form, could continue to provide a vehicle for helping disadvantaged students to position themselves competitively.

What Susan Church articulates so clearly is the impact on teachers of our current political world, the personal choice we all must make—whether to succumb to the conservative political agenda or to continue battling on behalf of children and students.

Susan lets us know what her choice is. She invites us to join the growing list of educators who "think and do 'the best things' in these difficult and challenging times" (123).

—Judith M. Newman

Acknowledgments

*W*oven through this book are the names of many individuals who have influenced my learning and writing over the years. Many others are not mentioned specifically, but I trust they know who they are.

Although Judith Newman figures prominently in this text and has written its foreword, that does not seem to be sufficient acknowledgment and thanks for her role in my life as teacher, colleague, and friend. Judith's departure from Nova Scotia to become Dean of the Faculty of Education at the University of Manitoba left a big hole in our literacy community and in my professional and personal life. While she still makes her presence felt through the phone, e-mail, and an occasional visit home, those connections feel tenuous when compared to the continual conversations that characterized our relationship when she lived close at hand. When I was immersed in writing this book, she and I sat over lunch one summer afternoon and talked through an early draft. It felt like old times. As usual, her comments and questions helped to make what seemed muddy to me much more clear. I want to thank her for that and for the countless other ways she has supported my learning and helped me to keep the laughter in my life.

More than ten years ago, when Judith first encouraged members of our literacy study group to publish our writing, we all reacted in disbelief. How could ordinary teachers like us become authors? She proved to us that we all could, in fact, write, and she helped us to become much more skilled and confident. But the group itself played an equally important part in that process. I am grateful that I can count most of those same people among my colleagues and friends today. Some have left Nova Scotia and some have drifted away from the group, but many still provide ongoing support, encouragement, and feedback, not only for me as a writer but also as a teacher and administrator. I particularly want to thank Margaret Swain, Kathleen Rosborough, Linda Swinwood, and Judy Mossip, who struggle with me to find new ways to teach, write, and lead.

There are many colleagues within the Halifax County–Bedford District School Board who continually help me sustain my belief that institutions can become less hierarchical, more collaborative, and more humane—despite much evidence to the contrary. They know when to be serious and when to laugh, and they seem to have an uncanny knack for calling just at the right time or for dropping in with a pink rose for my desk. These administrators and the many teachers I have come to know and respect for their dedication to students are the source of the optimism that I do have about the future of education.

I appreciate particularly the direct contribution of Linda Cook, Florence MacLean-Kanary, Jim Albright, Susan Settle, and Vivian Vasquez. They not only allowed me to include their stories in the book, but they also made time in their busy schedules to talk with me and to respond to early drafts as the text evolved.

Many teacher-educators have been an important part of my professional community. Within Mount Saint Vincent University, Andy Manning, Allan Neilsen, Lorri Neilsen, John Portelli, Blye Frank, Ursula Kelly, and Ann Vibert have helped to shape the perspectives that I share in this book. Jerry Harste has spent so much time in Nova Scotia over the years that he is part of our community. He has been generous in sharing his questions and insights and has helped us all to see both teaching and learning as inquiry. Pat Shannon and Carole Edelsky, while less frequent visitors, have had no less of an influence on me, as this book will show.

It was Toby Gordon, Publishing Director at Heinemann, who invited me to write this book. During our first conversation over breakfast, she neglected to mention that she planned for me to complete it in less than six months. Smart editor that she is, she hooked me first and discussed deadlines later. I have to admit there were times when I wondered why I ever agreed to the time line, especially as I sat in front of the computer during some of the precious warm and sunny days of a Nova Scotia summer. Although Toby and I were not in contact often, she was generous with her support, enthusiasm, and encouragement—all of which were needed at times. I want to thank her for the invitation to write and for being there along the way.

Finally, my love and thanks go to my husband, Don, for his unfailing support and interest in my work. He kept the computer running, the meals on the table, and the music in the air during several months of nonstop writing.

Preface

I seem to spend a great deal of my time these days defending aspects of education I value. Sometimes I engage in real arguments with people who disparage changes that I have actively promoted, such as critics who say that whole language is responsible for the inability of high school and college students to spell properly. More often, my conversations are imaginary. Recently I picked up the June 1995 issue of *The Council Chronicles*, the newsletter of the National Council of Teachers of English, which had been lying in my "to read" pile. A headline on the first page caught my eye: "State Standards-Setting Efforts Dogged by Politics." The accompanying article described how projects led by educators in several states had been undermined by politicians. Typical was a story from Idaho, where the State Superintendent ordered the draft of a "holistic, student-centered K–12 language arts framework" to be removed from circulation and replaced with a document that would describe in much more detail the specific skills to be taught. This action apparently was in aid of her pledge to "eradicate whole language methods and to return to a phonics-based approach to reading instruction" (8).

Stories from Michigan, Wisconsin, Montana, and Virginia, while different in the specifics, echoed similar themes: back-to-basics, heavy-handed political interference in the education agenda, and the use of a variety of tactics to undermine the efforts of educators to have a voice in shaping curricular directions. The reports from the various states were not entirely discouraging because, in every situation, articulate and knowledgeable educators were refusing to be silenced. Nevertheless, I found them decidedly disturbing. By the time I finished the article, I was furious and began envisioning conversations I could have with the politicians in question. I am getting used to being in that defensive mode. The experiences in those states reflect what has been happening across Canada—as the once strong movement toward whole language and related forms of progressive teaching is weakening as educators cope with often conflicting and contradictory agendas: back-to-basics, fiscal restraints, restructuring, site-based management, demands from the business community, and national and provincial testing.

During the years since I began teaching, I have positioned myself at various places along the progressive continuum. In particular, I have grown with and through whole language since the late 1970s. Today I feel a sense of urgency—not only about shoring up the gains we have made, but also about exploring both how we arrived at this juncture and how we might move forward from here. I have been concerned about whole language for some time, but it is only recently that I have seen it as vulnerable from threats without and, even more so, from problems within.

The challenges to whole language from without are the most obvious to see because they take shape in the open through media attacks, political actions, and general criticisms from those who focus on a perceived lack of attention to phonics, spelling, and other language skills. Much more complex, subtle, and thus more difficult to combat are the difficulties that have arisen from within as whole language has evolved.

I have seen whole language grow from a loosely coupled network of small groups of teachers and teacher-educators scattered across North America to a full-scale, sometimes disturbingly messianic, worldwide movement. As more and more individual teachers (and sometimes whole districts) embraced whole language, it became increasingly ill-defined and diverse. Now there are a wide range of beliefs and practices labeled whole language. Whole language means so many things to so many different people that it is in real danger of coming to mean nothing at all. Like many other whole language educators, I would like to disown some of what purports to be whole language teaching, but that is more difficult than it might seem. By calling myself a whole language educator, I seem to be stuck with all the baggage that the term has acquired over the years.

Our biggest difficulty seems to be in making the distinction between whole language as a movement and whole language as a philosophy. As Edelsky (1991) suggests, being part of a movement has been supportive to many teachers as they began to rethink their philosophies and practices; for most of us affiliation with a larger community helps to sustain our individual efforts. The problem with movements, however, is that they seem to spawn orthodoxies and surface understandings as new members enthusiastically become swept along. Whole language seems to have been particularly vulnerable to this. Several years ago, Judith Newman and I (1990) articulated a long series of "myths" that had become associated with whole language: there is no place for phonics, spelling, or grammar; teachers always facilitate and never teach directly; the classroom is unstructured; there is little evaluation; and on and on.

Now that whole language has gathered strength as a movement, it is a challenge to recast it as a perspective on teaching and learning. It is tempting to settle for simple solutions: if teachers just understood the philosophy better, we would not have all these problems. Obviously, that is part of the answer; many teachers need opportunities to learn more about working within a whole language framework. My concern is with how we keep that framework tentative and open as we attempt to promote change within the context of hierarchical institutions.

At the heart of the difficulties we have experienced with whole language is the widespread belief that it is about reaching certainties and naming final approaches to teaching rather than about exploring doubts and asking ever-changing questions. I want to disassociate myself from the popular versions of whole language that suggest it is just another methodology with points that can be contrasted, usually unfavorably by its many critics, with approaches that have a more evident emphasis on skills. I despair when I read articles that make whole language seem as if it is only successful with bright, middle-class students who come well-versed in school language and ready to embrace literacy in "natural" settings. I wonder why some who espouse whole language paint literacy development as neat, simple, and "nice" when I recognize how messy, complicated, and conflicted it is.

Central to my theory of whole language is the understanding that it is complex and open-ended. This is what makes it so generative and powerful, but it is also what seems to have been lost in the transformation of whole language into a movement. Movements by their very nature seem to be long on answers and short on questions. I believe that whole language educators have been insufficiently aware of the power that social context has in shaping teachers' interpretations of whole language. Specifically, I believe that many of our well-intentioned attempts to support the growth of whole language within school systems have contributed to our current difficulties. It is difficult, if not impossible, to foster tentative thinking within an institution that values right answers. I also believe that we have paid too little attention to the political implications of whole language—that we have shied away from grappling with difficult and complex issues of power and control, especially in contexts beyond the classroom.

I want to bring the political questions to the fore as a means of sustaining whole language. Clearly, we need to become more politically aware if we are to counteract the attacks from without that increasingly are being played out in the political arena. More important, we need to understand that whole language embodies a particular political stance. As Harman and Edelsky (1989) argue, "the most powerful of [whole language] beliefs and practices—and therefore the most liberating and potentially alienating—is the whole language commitment to a democratic relationship both between the student and the teacher, and between the student and the material" (397). Since most classrooms and the institution as a whole reflect authoritarian beliefs and practices, making a shift to whole language means taking up this political agenda, which has always been implicit within whole language but too rarely has been made explicit.

By keeping the political agenda hidden, we diminish the likelihood that whole language will reach its potential as a force for social change. Instead, it will continue to be seen as just another methodology for teaching reading and writing. By ignoring the political, we also cut off productive avenues of inquiry into why and how the process of enacting whole language philosophy is so problematic. By taking up that political agenda, we raise questions of a different order than, Should we teach phonics? Political questions such as the following are what interest me:

- Why and how has whole language been subverted within hierarchical institutions?
- How have my own position and ways of working within the institution contributed to the problems with enacting whole language philosophy?
- How should my theories and practices change to become more reflective of my commitment to democratic ideals of equity and social justice?
- How can I support the continuing growth of teachers toward a more overtly political version of whole language?
- How can thoughtful whole language educators critique whole language as a movement and yet sustain it as a philosophy?
- Is it possible to reinvent whole language or does it carry too much baggage?

Much of this book is about what it could mean to make whole language more consciously political.

∿∿∿ Introduction

An Expanding Theory of Learning

*A*lthough this book as a whole reflects my current theoretical perspectives on whole language, critical theory, and politics, I think it is important for readers to be clear from the outset about what I mean when I use those terms.

Beliefs About Learning

I have thought, written, and talked so much about whole language over the years that it should be easy for me to explain what it means. Instead, I find that there is such a complex array of attitudes, beliefs, and practices associated with my current understandings of whole language, that it has become increasingly difficult for me to define it simply and briefly. Moreover, I have seen how attempts by whole language educators (including me) to offer simple and brief definitions have resulted in myths, misconceptions and orthodoxies. Therefore, instead of offering a definition, I present a list of the underlying beliefs about learning that provide the underpinnings for all my work. Although the individual beliefs are separated and sequentially ordered on this list, in my mind they are inseparable, mutually supportive, and interconnected.

1. *Learners actively construct meaning by relating new information to their prior knowledge.* As a teacher, I assume that learners come with a broad range of experiences and insights that will shape their future learning. Within the learning

situation, I structure many opportunities for them to draw upon and share these prior understandings and to explore how new information relates to what they already know.

2. *Learning occurs through the active involvement of learners in generating and testing hypotheses, seeing patterns and relationships, and making connections.* As a teacher, I invite experimentation and encourage learners to inquire into questions that interest them. I know that learners' early attempts at something new will be approximate and marked by errors, and I help them move forward by learning from their mistakes.

3. *The learner's purposes and intentions determine how, when, and what learning occurs.* No matter how skilled and talented I might be as a teacher, my success depends upon my learners' seeing reasons to learn. Therefore, I need to know who they are as people; to understand and value their interests, desires, and goals; to try to connect learning to their lives; to offer them choices; and to actively engage them in directing their own learning.

4. *Learning occurs through the learner's direct involvement in and reflections upon a wide range of experiences.* Said another way, learners learn by doing and by thinking about what they are doing. As a teacher, I immerse children in complex, whole and integrated experiences, and I build in many opportunities for them to reflect, both individually and collectively, upon how they are learning. Along the way I offer feedback, encouragement, support, and information, as needed.

5. *Learning is social.* This seemingly simple belief carries with it a wide range of implications. Because we live and learn in social contexts, the meanings we construct are shaped by the social groups to which we belong. From the moment we are born, we learn through our interactions with others. As a teacher, I try to create a learning community in which learners have many opportunities to interact, to share their diverse perspectives, and to learn from each other. I work to make the learning community inclusive by inviting the

2

participation of all: students, teachers, administrators, parents, and other adults. Within this social learning environment, there is ongoing negotiation of power and control. Teachers and learners work to develop social relationships that reflect democratic principles.

I believe that educators who are committed to the development of whole language curriculum need to create their own belief statements and to build both their theories and practices around the elements outlined above.

Essential Elements of Whole Language Theory

The following elements evolve from my beliefs. Taken as a whole, they constitute the knowledge base that underlies my practices as a whole language educator.

The Learning Context

An essential aspect of teaching from a whole language perspective is structuring both the physical and social environments to foster social interaction and mental and physical activity. To create this supportive learning context, teachers

- organize time and space to facilitate engaging all learners in complex experiences;
- provide learners with opportunities to work on their own and with others;
- encourage members of the learning community to collaboratively develop structures and expectations that help them live and work together in harmony;
- invite learners to establish routines, procedures, and responsibilities together; and
- encourage students to share diverse perspectives, to consider different opinions, and to resolve conflicts when necessary.

The Roles of the Teacher

In these learning contexts, teachers clearly have special roles. As they begin to work with each new group of learners, they establish initial expectations, plan experiences and invite participation. They offer what Smith (1981) termed "demonstrations," which he defined as opportunities for learners to see how something is done. For example, teachers who read and write in the classroom demonstrate how experienced readers and writers deal with texts. As students take on more responsibility for their own learning, teachers continue to be actively involved in helping to shape directions. In particular, they

- create learning experiences that they think will support students' continuing growth;
- pose questions, ask for opinions and ideas, and offer their own perspectives;
- monitor each student's learning and provide support and input as needed;
- decide when to provide focused instruction that will help individuals or groups to move forward;
- carry out ongoing observations and assessments and use the information they gather to give feedback to learners, to plan future instruction, and to report students' progress to parents and administrators;
- and engage in ongoing reflection regarding learning and teaching.

The Language Systems

To work within a whole language philosophy, teachers need to know about language. The more we know, the better able we are to support each learner's growth as a language user. A central understanding is that language, whether oral or written, is composed of four interrelated and interdependent systems. Our knowledge of these language systems helps us to make informed observations as children talk, read, and write and it allows us to determine how best to support their further development. The language systems are as follows:

- The *pragmatic system* refers to how the context influences the ways language is used and interpreted. The context can be as broad as the overall situation or the social relationships among the language users, and it can be as narrow as the text within which a sentence or word occurs. Our pragmatic knowledge helps us know what to expect. For example, as an experienced reader I can predict the style and type of material I will encounter in a novel as opposed to that of a textbook. Because I have participated in many different kinds of social groups, I know that speaking to colleagues at a meeting is different from speaking to them at a staff party.
- The *semantic system* refers to the complex of meanings in a language. The meanings language users bring to oral and written language are influenced by their prior experiences and cultural backgrounds. For example, the word *farm* in a text will mean something different to a young child growing up in the midst of the dairy country of Wisconsin than it will to a child who lives on a small vegetable farm in New England or Nova Scotia.
- The *syntactic system* is the set of rules that regulates the relationship between words, sentences, and paragraphs. It includes word order, tense, number, and gender. For example, I use my knowledge of syntax when I add *ed* to a verb to show that something occurred in the past.
- The *phonological system* (in oral language) refers to the relationships between sounds in a language. The *grapho-phonic system* (in written language) refers to the set of relationships between the sounds and the written forms of the language. We use our knowledge of grapho-phonics to help us pronounce words we read and to translate what we hear into written form.

Language Processes

Children learn language by using it in many different situations. They learn to orchestrate a range of meaning-making strategies in increasingly complex ways. In addition to knowing about the language systems, teachers need to understand these language learning processes. From the broad range of research literature available in this area, it seems important to mention aspects that have made a special contribution to our understanding of literacy learning and teaching. Those aspects include the following:

- Inquiry into how readers orchestrate a range of strategies and cuing systems as they read (Goodman, Watson, and Burke 1987);
- The research related to writing as process (Graves 1983, 1994; Murray 1982; Calkins 1991, 1995; and many others) and reading/writing connections (Hansen 1987; Harwayne 1992; and others);
- Work in the area of reader response (Rosenblatt 1978; Probst 1988; Short and Pierce 1990; Chambers 1985, 1993; and others); and
- Research related to the role of talk in learning (Barnes 1976; Tough 1985; Booth and Thornley-Hall 1991a, 1991b; Pierce and Gilles 1993; and others).

Language and Other Communication Systems

At one time, literacy educators focused primarily on oral and written language, but it is now incumbent upon us to learn more about how learners come to know through the visual arts, drama, music, movement, and mathematics. In the information age, we need to be informed about media literacy and the role of technology. I believe whole language education must include opportunities for learners to construct and communicate meaning in many different ways and to explore the interrelationships between communication systems.

Connections Across the Curriculum

In my view, whole language philosophy underlies the entire curriculum, not just what occurs in the language arts class. Inquiries in social studies, science, and mathematics provide contexts within which learners can pursue questions that interest them, engage in many purposeful experiences, use language and other communication systems for learning, and make connections with the world outside the classroom. In addition, there are many opportunities for curriculum integration as learners explore topics from a number of different perspectives. For example, learners might investigate pollution through scientific explorations, through the analysis of statistical information, through fiction and nonfiction texts, and through the eyes of a painter or photographer.

Insights From Critical Theory

As my understanding of whole language continues to grow and change, from time to time I transform my theoretical framework by adding new elements that I had not previously considered. Most recently, I have incorporated insights from critical theory that I believe greatly enhance the potential of whole language to promote positive social change.

In particular, as I reflected on the perspectives of several critical theorists (Giroux 1987; Simon 1987; Giroux and McLaren 1986; McLaren 1989) and of whole language educators such as Edelsky (1991, 1994), I expanded my perception that learning is social and came to see social learning as the underlying foundation of all whole language beliefs. I recognized the profound influence of the social context on the individual's construction of meaning and use of language, and I realized the naivete of some of my earlier notions about the reader's personal interpretations of text or the writer's expression of voice.

Critical theory helped me to understand that interpretations and expressions are never simply personal. Instead, they are caught up in a network of social relationships based upon race, class, gender, culture, ability, and other characteristics through which the individual's positions in society are defined. Every individual occupies a number of different positions based upon membership in various social groups that express their differences through *discourse*. When individuals acquire the discourse of a social group, they learn how to speak and act in ways that distinguish them from other groups.

Fundamental to this theory is the understanding that our society is organized in ways that create unequal relationships among social groups and the discourses associated with them. Those with the most power and privilege occupy positions of dominance over others—so much so that their values, beliefs, and perspectives define what is normal or regular in society. The discourse of the dominant group is privileged and becomes the ideal to which all must aspire if they hope to gain full participation in society. Therefore, learning language and learning through language is not just a psychological process but also a sociological process; language both reflects and perpetuates social relationships. Dominant discourses are taken for granted as the "way things are supposed to be." Because our institutions and social practices are controlled by dominant groups, they are structured to sustain the existing power relationships. Giroux (1987) defines schools not just as instructional sites but as cultural sites that

> generate and embody support for particular forms of culture as is evident in the school's support for specific ways of speaking, the legitimating of distinct forms of knowledge, the privileging of certain histories and patterns of authority, and the confirmation of particular ways of experiencing and seeing the world. (176)

Critical theorists argue that those who believe in social justice and equity must not only understand the relationships between power and language but also use language to critique and to subvert the existing unequal power relationships—to uncover the problems that exist in "the way things are supposed to be." To take a critical approach to teaching means to make issues of power and privilege central. It means the teacher involves learners in working toward social justice and equity within the classroom, and thus puts the problems of living together in a democracy at the center of the curriculum rather than at the periphery. It means structuring a context within which participants are free to express and consider diverse perspectives and points of view, but within which these perspectives are also the focus of critique. For example, critical teachers help learners to examine the assumptions that underlie racist, classist, or sexist perspectives and to ask questions when power is used to coerce or to dominate. These teachers encourage students to move beyond connecting texts to their personal experiences to consider how text interpretation is grounded in the social—in gender, race, class, culture, and in the student's, teacher's, and author's assumptions about the world (Edelsky 1991, 165). Critical teachers support students' use of language to act on the world, such as, to speak or write about social issues or injustices in an effort to effect change.

Although some critical theorists (Willinsky 1990; Giroux 1987) have aimed their critique at whole language and other forms of progressive teaching because of the perceived focus on the personal and individual, my reading of critical theory suggests that there is nothing incompatible between whole language theory and critical teaching. The learning beliefs I outlined above can easily accommodate a move to a more critical version of whole language through an expanded understanding of learning as social. In fact, it is through becoming more critical that whole language will reach its potential.

A Word About Politics

In Edelsky's (1991) words, "Whole Language is not only a pedagogy that just happens to have political consequences; it is also a pedagogy with a political stance; i.e., Whole Language opposes social stratification and promotes an egalitarian social order" (164). This political stance seems to have gotten lost in the majority of the versions of whole language that have evolved through the movement. It seems that many educators are uneasy about the prospect of becoming explicitly political. I was quite far along in my own career before I realized that it was impossible to be apolitical—that everything I say and do represents a political stance, whether or not I make it explicit. As a member of society, I live and work within a network of power relationships that are negotiated through politics. If I remain silent about social injustices or inequities, that is as much a political stance as if I choose to speak or act to effect change. If I allow others to make decisions that adversely affect the lives of my students or my own working conditions without protest, I am implicated in those decisions. Ignoring issues of gender, class, race, and culture in my work with students and adults is as political as bringing them to the fore. As Shannon (1992) tells us, "All teachers are political, whether they are conscious of it or not. Their acts contribute to or challenge the status quo in literacy education, in schools, and in society" (2).

I suppose I was more comfortable when I thought I could be apolitical, yet it was very much like living with blinders on. I experienced and observed the effects of unequal power relationships in society, but I did not understand my own role in perpetuating them and did not view myself as having the capacity to change them. I was well into adulthood before I realized that my perspectives as a member of the nondominant gender had legitimacy—that I did not have to adopt male ways of knowing and being to "count" as a member of society. Even more troubling to me now, however, is realizing that many other inequities were completely invisible to me because of my position of relative privilege in society; as a member of the dominant white middle class, I saw many social practices, including schooling, as givens. Although I became a teacher because I thought I could make a difference in students' lives, I did not understand how the institution I became a part of disempowers learners and teachers. As a product of that institution, I was ill-equipped to bring a political analysis to my work.

I believe educators who choose to become explicitly political have the potential to transform schooling so that our students gain the first-hand experience with democracy that most of us lacked in our own education. I believe we must foster critical literacy skills through which students can both analyze and act to change the social practices that perpetuate inequalities and injustices. As Shannon (1993) urges, we can "move ourselves and our students from our original position of seeing ourselves as *objects* who believe that economics, politics, and schooling happen to us, to a new position of seeing ourselves as *subjects*, who have the right, ability and responsibility to participate in the decision making that affects our lives" (91). Becoming overtly political has its risks, but continuing to live with the blinders on is even more risky, especially in the current political and social context. As I continue to learn about and recognize the complexities and challenges that taking up a political agenda presents, I also am becoming more aware that through this means, we *can* make a difference.

☰ Chapter One

Coming Full Circle

*A*s an undergraduate university student in the 1960s, I became enthralled with the social sciences, especially cultural anthropology. Many of my friends had already decided on sensible and marketable majors such as nursing, teaching, and social work, and they looked askance at the reading assignments that fascinated me: ethnographies of the Tlingits and Haidas of northwestern North America and of many different African tribes; studies of kinship systems and rites of passage; and theoretical perspectives on language and culture. As I was about to graduate with a major in anthropology, my father, a successful businessman who had lived and worked for many years in New York City, commented, "With that and five cents, you can get a ride on the Staten Island Ferry!"

There really wasn't much I *could* do with that degree. Like many females raised in the 1950s and early 1960s, I got married a few days after I graduated and was not prepared to travel to pursue graduate work in anthropology. Instead, I decided to increase my chances of becoming gainfully employed by enrolling in a teacher education program. It was there that I first encountered the ideas of Dewey (1938, 1944), Bruner (1960), Holt (1964), Postman and Weingartner (1969), and other progressive educators. I now know that the philosophical perspective I began to develop through the readings and discussions in my courses was quite consistent with what I much later came to understand as whole language. At that time, my focus had nothing to do with literacy education; I was preparing to teach social studies, and nowhere in my program did anyone suggest that I would need to know anything about language and literacy to help my students learn history or geography. It wasn't until my first year of teaching that I discovered how woefully inadequate my preparation was for what faced me in a seventh-grade American History classroom in a small town in Rhode Island.

I embarked on my career with much idealism. I envisioned myself inspiring my students with experiential learning, opportunities for inquiry, and projects that would engage their minds. I remembered how boring and mind-numbing I had found most of my schooling, despite the fact that I had always done well. I vowed to be a different kind of teacher. I saw myself enacting curriculum based upon progressive notions, such as Dewey's (1938) emphasis on student participation in directing the learning process.

Like many first-year teachers, I had little idea how I could put any of this into practice. I carefully planned open-ended activities, but the students had no prior experience with that kind of teaching. They did not know how to work together or how to direct their own learning. Moreover, they had no use for my new methods. Before long, most of my classes were out of control. The students were grouped by ability, and so some of the groups included few students who were capable of working independently. In the most difficult class, not one student could make any sense of the textbook and most could barely write a sentence. Even the most able group balked at my progressive approaches. When I gave an assignment related to the Bill of Rights that required students to apply some of the principles to their own lives, the phone rang off the wall with complaints from parents who could not understand the assignment.

Recognizing that I was going under, the principal and the department head spent days in my classroom helping me to restore order. They and the more experienced teachers on staff advised me to abandon my bright ideas about experiential learning and to take control through teacher-directed activities. Another social studies teacher suggested simplified reading material and worksheets for my most unruly class. Later, I discovered that the veteran teachers had saddled me with the two worst classes in the school because I was a newcomer—another early lesson for me in the politics of schooling.

Somehow I survived that year. I learned to impose order and to be a good disciplinarian. I adopted the methods all the other teachers were using. Even after I regained control of the classroom, however, I knew that I was not meeting my students' needs. I still believed in progressive ideals, but I could see no way to actualize them. Greatly disillusioned, I was actually quite relieved when my husband was transferred and I had to give up that teaching job. In the next few years we moved several times, and I only made half-hearted attempts to find employment in teaching. I did some substituting and applied my newly developed disciplinary skills. I found jobs outside education, and took time off to travel.

Eventually we moved to Fredericton, New Brunswick, and I decided it was long past time for me to get serious about my career. Although there were no teaching positions available, the local school district was looking for volunteers to assist students with learning problems. I became a volunteer tutor and enrolled in reading methods courses at the local university. The memory of how badly I had failed those students in Rhode Island still stung, and I was determined to learn more about how to help children who were struggling with literacy.

Over the next couple of years, my volunteer work grew to a part-time, and soon a full-time, position as a remedial teacher. Through university courses and district inservices, I learned how to teach phonics, sight vocabulary, and literal and inferential comprehension. I participated in the phase in the learning disabilities movement when experts believed that children needed training in visual and auditory perception to ready them for reading. I remember leading struggling readers and writers through tracing exercises, puzzles and games to improve their visual skills, and through auditory training activities designed to help them hear subtle differences in words. As part of our repertoire, we used texts that were called *linguistic readers* to supplement the skills-based basal readers being used in the classroom. These texts were made up entirely of regularly patterned words to train students systematically and sequentially in automatic word recognition. The books contained no illustrations, because the idea was to focus total attention on the print. The simplest "stories" repeated words of one syllable, such as, "Dan can fan Nan." Gradually, the texts became more complex by adding articles, other sight words, and patterned words of more than one syllable; they never became much more meaningful.

During that period, classroom and remedial teachers paid almost no attention to writing; lessons in usage and spelling and occasional opportunities for creative writing seemed to constitute most classroom writing programs. Much writing consisted of children's answers to comprehension questions which, of course, had to be in complete sentences.

I cannot remember seeing any contradiction between my progressive beliefs about learning and my practices as a remedial teacher. Possibly it was because most of what I learned about teaching reading focused on practice. I have no recollection of anyone suggesting in any of my courses or inservices that the methods I was learning were grounded in a theoretical framework. I saw no connection between what Dewey said about learning and what I might do in the name of literacy instruction. I was not, however, totally convinced that the approaches I was using were really helping my students learn to read. Most of them had difficulty coping with their classroom reading programs and struggled to make sense of phonics and other skills. Some of them became quite good at rhyming from the pattern drills in remedial lessons, but few of them seemed to be able to pick up even a simple book and read it for pleasure.

In the mid-1970s, I embarked on a journey that led me back to my progressive roots and, eventually, to whole language philosophy. That journey began with an experience that, for me, became what Judith Newman (1987) terms a "critical incident"—a happening that caused me to ask myself, "What's going on here?" During a keynote address at a reading conference, Frank Smith challenged the current notions about teaching by stating, "Systematic instruction is the systematic deprivation of experience." Many in the audience were angry, and I recall that I was none too pleased to have my own methods so sharply criticized. Yet a few weeks later, I had reason to reconsider Smith's assertion. As I was reading with Jeff, one of the students who was slowly making his way through the first level of linguistic readers, he encountered the word *hut*. Jeff had no difficulty with pronounciation, having read *cut*, *but*, *nut*, *mutt*, etc.; however, he turned and asked me what it meant. Clearly, there was no point in directing him back to the text; there were no illustrations and virtually no contextual clues. I tried in vain to trigger some bit of background knowledge through discussion, and then I ended up making a crude sketch by way of explanation.

That experience was a real-life demonstration of what Smith had been saying about systematic instruction. It also demonstrated the important role of nonvisual information in reading. Tentatively, I began to explore what Smith (1971, 1978), Goodman (1967), and others were writing about the reading process. In 1979 I moved to Nova Scotia and began hearing about Judith Newman, who had just completed a doctoral program with Frank Smith and had returned to the province to teach at Dalhousie University. The stories painted Judith as a radical thinker who had the reading education community up in arms with her critiques of the dominant skills-based instruction. Aided and abetted by David Doake, a teacher educator at Acadia University, Judith was challenging teachers' long-held assumptions about literacy learning and teaching. I decided that Judith was just the person I needed to get to know, so I eagerly enrolled in a summer workshop she was leading in collaboration with a number of teachers who had been studying with her.

There, Judith and the teachers expanded on Smith's notions of visual and nonvisual information, showing how teachers might build curriculum around new theories of reading development. For the first time, I learned about miscue analysis and began to think about reading in terms of cuing systems and strategies. We spent hours in small groups listening to a taped reading over and over, and struggling to learn the miscue coding system. Since most of us were accustomed to using traditional reading assessments that judged performance on speed and accuracy, this was unfamiliar new territory. The teacher-leaders also conducted hands-on sessions to show what they were doing in their classrooms. Their excitement was contagious as they led us through experiences with Big Books, predictable texts, strategies such as brainstorming and categorizing information to organize projects, and many other approaches. I left the workshop determined both to apply what I had learned to my own teaching and to learn more.

The next fall I enrolled in a course with Judith and soon became part of a growing community of teachers attempting to make change in their classrooms. Looking back on these first few years of the growth of what came to be known as "whole language," I can see that the strength came from small groups of teachers reflecting on their beliefs and practices under the guidance of a leader who continually challenged us to ground instruction in a theoretical framework. Clearly, our prime concern was what we were going to *do* in our classrooms, but Judith's insistence that we reflect on *why* we chose certain activities over others and on *how* those choices affected our learners moved us beyond the development of new practices to an ongoing rethinking of our beliefs. It was an exciting time to be a teacher. Together, we saw endless possibilities for transforming our classrooms.

We pushed our thinking further when we began exploring the relationships between reading and writing. We discovered the work of Graves (1983), Murray (1982), Calkins (1983), and many of their colleagues who began publishing articles in professional journals. We read Smith (1982); Harste, Woodward, and Burke (1984); and supported Judith through the process of writing and publishing her first book (Newman 1984a), a close look at young children's writing. We became writers ourselves, and one of the study groups evolved into a writing group. Many of us wrote about cross-curricular applications of our theories of learning. It became obvious to us that our inquiry into literacy learning was much broader than we had originally thought; it went far beyond the teaching of reading and writing to the development of a framework of beliefs about teaching and learning. Our sense of ourselves as professionals grew with the publication of a collection of our articles (Newman 1984b).

I cannot remember when we first began using the term "whole language." It did appear in the title of our book, so it must have been some time in the early 1980s. In the introduction to that book, Judith included a summary of whole language beliefs: She wrote about the social nature of learning, about risk-taking and student choice, about the teacher's role as facilitator and supporter, and about the importance of integrated literacy instruction.

Those were radical notions for the time, as was Judith's emphasis on theory: "The more we know about how language operates and how students learn, the easier it is to recognize materials which on the surface look like whole language, but actually fall short. We've realized that for instruction to be coherent, it must be based on a conceptual framework" (1994b, 5).

The expansion of my own conceptual framework drew me back to the progressive philosophies that had framed my initial teacher education program. I even began to make connections with my undergraduate studies in anthropology as ethnographic research carried out in educational contexts began to appear in the literature. I hauled out college texts related to culture and language and read them with new questions in mind—questions that emerged from my struggles to make sense of my students' learning. Unlike my first year of teaching, however, when I floundered on my own, I now had support in the challenging task of building curriculum from those theories. I felt that I had truly come full circle, not quite returning to where I had started, but bringing to those basic beliefs a perspective that was informed by my prior negative experiences with instruction based on the notion that learning occurs through the mastery of a sequential series of skills. Now I could critically contrast my work with struggling readers and writers in both the old and new contexts, and I could see for myself that students made more progress when I shifted the focus from the decoding and encoding of print to the making of meaning (Church 1984). More important, I had a theory to explain the differences in the outcomes.

ᨡᨡᨡ Chapter Two

Institutionalizing Whole Language

*B*y the mid-1980s, whole language in Nova Scotia had changed from a grass-roots movement of university faculty and classroom teachers to a province-wide phenomenon. The provincial Department of Education, which has responsibility for curriculum development, published a new guideline, *Language Arts in the Elementary School* (1986). This guideline mandated programming consistent with "an integrated approach and a holistic perspective" (1). Both the Department and school districts initiated activities to promote the implementation of this new program framework. In my own district, changes had already been occurring through inservice activities and a shift from skills-based basal readers to integrated language arts series, newly published by several Canadian publishers. The publication of the guideline gave added impetus to these efforts.

A number of us who had been working with teacher educators such as Judith became leaders in this implementation effort. We conducted countless inservices at the school and district levels and at local and provincial conferences. Other leaders in the whole language movement visited the province as well, not only to make presentations and conduct workshops, but to visit our whole language classrooms. When I attended the IRA national conference in 1985, I was surprised to learn that Nova Scotia was gaining an international reputation as a leader in whole language.

As a result, visitors from afar came expecting to see whole language teaching in every classroom in the province. However, the reality was far from that. Teachers accustomed to working with sequential basal programs struggled to use literature-based series to teach reading. Told to abandon ability grouping, they introduced many whole class experiences and attempted to create flexible groups, but they often found this difficult to organize. At the same time, they developed much more extensive writing programs, attempting to implement what came to be known as "writing process" instruction, but without a clear understanding of why they were being asked to change or how they could incorporate these changes in their classrooms. While there was *some* focus on the theory underlying these changes, for the most part inservices only dealt with the procedures for new practices. In my own district, all teachers attended a series of centrally planned inservices that were conducted over two years. Topics included reading process, writing process, reading/writing connections, and evaluation. The leaders of these sessions tried to frame the sessions in theory, such as providing background information on the work of Smith and of Goodman, but the information was too sketchy and fragmented to be meaningful to the teachers, most of whom were totally unfamiliar with these new ideas. Moreover, most teachers in the province who had relied on basal reading series to guide instruction for many years saw no purpose in learning about theory. They wanted to know precisely what they were now supposed to do in their classrooms.

By the late 1980s, the pace of inservice activity slowed, and many districts shifted emphasis to other areas of the curriculum. The officially sanctioned implementation was complete. Some teachers recognized how much they still had to learn and continued to seek out opportunities for professional development through university courses, study groups, and their own professional reading. Most, unfortunately, were left with a new set of practices (such as Big Books, semantic webbing, reading and writing conferences, and so on), but little understanding of the theory of learning upon which these new practices were based. There was widespread outward compliance with the provincial and district change directives, but a great deal of subtle, and sometimes not so subtle, resistance among teachers. By that time I had taken a position as a curriculum supervisor, and I can remember dropping in on classrooms unexpectedly and finding old-style phonics lessons in full swing. The greeting from the teacher was usually a version of, "I know I am not supposed to be doing this, but . . ." At the other extreme were classrooms in which there seemed to be very little teacher direction—in which teachers seemed to have backed right out of the classroom. There were many whole language types of activities in place, but there seemed to be little sense of purpose behind them. A knowledgeable whole language teacher once described this to me as "whole language dress up."

Through my work with teachers, it soon became apparent to me that we were in real trouble. Parents had also begun complaining about the perceived, and sometimes real, lack of attention to phonics, spelling, and grammar. While many parents seemed to accept "invented spelling" in first grade, they began to ask questions when children still seemed to be making many mistakes after three or four years in school. Parents frequently asked me, "Why do you let them make mistakes? If they learned it right in the first place, they wouldn't be making all these mistakes." Many teachers could not explain their new ways of teaching to the satisfaction of parents, so community confidence waned even further. A major backlash seemed to be building among both teachers and parents. Camps began to form, with whole language advocates and their critics firmly lined up on opposite sides of every issue related to literacy teaching and learning.

I was concerned for two reasons: I saw competent whole language teachers coming under fire because of the general backlash, and I saw too many children not progressing as readers and writers in classrooms with teachers who lacked the background knowledge necessary to develop effective whole language curriculum.

When the district asked me to write a guideline for the language arts curriculum from grades four through nine, I jumped at this chance to address the problems I saw. By that time I was very much aware of the inadequacies of curriculum guides and traditional forms of inservice, so I was determined to take a different approach. To begin, I formed a committee of administrators and teachers who I knew shared my concerns about how curriculum change in language arts was unfolding in the district. We met over the course of nearly a year to read, talk, and write about literacy issues in a learning environment very much like a whole language classroom. We crafted a series of scenarios that portrayed teachers building curriculum based on whole language theory. To address the issue of skills, we demonstrated how teachers could draw attention to spelling and grammar within the context of writing. Hoping to dispel the notion that whole language means less teacher involvement, we painted portraits of active, reflective, engaged teachers. These teachers were very much still in the classroom, not only responding to students, but initiating, planning, structuring, questioning, and offering information and insights, as needed. We invited students and other teachers to write about their experiences, as well.

In an effort to create a document that would be invitational rather than directive, we published this writing, not as a curriculum guide, but as a book, *From Teacher to Teacher: Opening Our Doors* (Church 1989). We launched it with great enthusiasm, inviting district staff to join us in celebrating the accomplishments of its many authors. The press picked up on the story and reported favorably on this unusual teacher resource that described classrooms so unlike the ones the reporters had experienced in their days in school. Committee members developed plans for facilitating discussions around the book within their own schools. We eagerly waited for the responses to our work to come, but, to our disappointment and chagrin, the publication caused barely a ripple. Most administrators and teachers ignored it. When there was a response, it was often in the form of negative comments toward the teacher-authors, many of whom later described their own feelings of alienation and anger (Church, 1992).

The teachers and I had many conversations about this experience, which we simply came to call *Opening Our Doors.* Ironically, this experiment seemed to close more doors than it opened.

Committee members and others who had been involved felt very positive about the experience, so why had it fallen so flat when we attempted to move beyond our group? It was more than a year later before I was ready to "conduct research on myself" (Newman 1987) by critically reflecting on this incident. As part of a 1990 summer course with Patrick Shannon, I was able to bring a political analysis to the experience through an article that I wrote for class (Shannon 1992). Through course readings, discussion, and writings, Patrick led participants to consider these questions:

Why are the dominating sides of literacy, teaching and schooling more often practiced than the liberating sides?
Why is it that, despite the rhetoric that education is the backbone of democracy, participants in schooling have so little voice in matters of consequence in the classroom?
Why are they so unfree?
Who is really served by the current organization and practice of schools?
How can the liberating sides of literacy, teaching and schooling be realized? (Shannon 1992, 3)

In addition to Shannon's questions, the writings of some of the critical theorists (Giroux 1987; Giroux and McLaren 1986; Simon 1987; Trimbur 1989) offered me another way to conceptualize the history of whole language in Nova Scotia. Reading and discussing these writings in a formal and focused way provided me with a new framework to reflect on my role in the curriculum change effort—in particular, on my role in the unsuccessful *Opening Our Doors* project. I realized I needed to situate my own experiences within a broader analysis of institutional change initiatives as they are typically practiced within hierarchical organizations. I needed to look and listen beyond the critical, unkind comments other staff members had made and to try to understand the source of the anger and bitterness. I began to see that teachers who were not included in the select group that helped form my project saw the publication as a threat that could further disempower them.

When I asked teachers how they viewed their initial introduction to whole language, the majority reported feeling threatened, intimidated, confused, and powerless. The inservices left them with the impression that everything they had done in the past was wrong. Most of them recalled that workshop leaders had explained whole language by comparing it to a skills-based model, sometimes through charts with contrasting descriptors: focus on meaning vs. focus on skills; whole-to-part learning vs. part-to-whole learning; skills developed as part of meaningful whole vs. skills developed sequentially; etc. Overwhelmingly, teachers believed that they had been told to let the learning unfold naturally, to avoid direct teaching, to dispense with the teaching of phonics and spelling, and to trust "the process." When they attempted to follow through on these directives and many children did not progress as readers and writers, they blamed whole language. One of my colleagues recalled her frustration at not knowing why she was being asked to change, yet having to try to incorporate new methods. She later enrolled in university courses and developed a theory base to support the new practices, but she is convinced that it would have been impossible for her to teach from a whole language perspective with only the knowledge she gained from the district-sponsored staff development.

While some of these teachers reported that they resisted the change by refusing to abandon practices that they felt had been effective in the past, such as phonics instruction, few of them felt safe to voice their opposition openly. As I reflected on my own leadership role, I recognized that I had not invited dialogue within the context of staff development experiences. There were few opportunities for teachers to question why they were being asked to change when they believed they were already doing a competent job. In working with the teachers, I had been guilty of perpetuating practices that controlled and silenced teachers—at the very same time I was promoting the development of student voice, choice, and self-direction within their classrooms. Ironically, the top-down effort to institutionalize whole language, and thus to liberate students from the shackles of traditional teacher-directed instruction, resulted in many teachers feeling disempowered, angry, and anything but liberated.

It was into that troubled context that we dropped our *Opening Our Doors* project, naively thinking that the audience would see it as something different from previous attempts to promote whole language. Clearly, we underestimated how powerfully the teachers' prior experiences and the hierarchical institution itself would shape the book's reception in the district. The majority of teachers in our audience saw the book as another curriculum guide designed to direct their work—more right answers to questions they hadn't even asked—and they reacted accordingly. They brought a number of preconceptions to this curriculum change process: system publications by definition are directives, so we will ignore this one like most others; talking with other teachers about our work might show our inadequacies, so we will avoid it; we are in competition with each other for the few rewards available in the organization, and these teacher-authors are getting too many of them; this book is just more experts trying to tell us how to do whole language.

At the same time, the teachers involved in the project bore the brunt of this rejection and negativity. They felt silenced, not only by their colleagues, but by the institution. They wanted to engage in professional conversations with teachers on their staffs, but they recognized that they were perceived as a threat. They created classroom contexts within which their learners were empowered, but they were keenly aware of their own lack of power to influence decision-making in the institution. For example, when they attempted to voice their concerns about important issues such as teaching loads, schedules, and evaluation, school and district-level administrators failed even to respond, much less to give their perspectives serious consideration.

My efforts to apply my whole language principles in my work with the teacher-authors involved creating a liberatory context and providing opportunities for their voices to be heard. However, when the project activity moved beyond that group, it became much more difficult to establish supportive learning contexts for other teachers. In our eagerness to share what we had learned, we inadvertently created a change process that looked and felt very much like a top-down, authoritarian, one-size-fits-all implementation.

As a result of all my experiences with promoting change, I have come to the conclusion that the "implementation of whole language" is really an oxymoron. We cannot use coercive tactics to promote a liberatory belief system. Yet those of us who work in hierarchical institutions, such as the public school system, often find ourselves perpetuating the very practices we know are contradictory to what we believe. Therefore, promoting a whole language perspective means moving beyond discussions of classroom teaching; learning to raise critical questions about institutional structures, practices, and relationships; and envisioning alternative ways of living and working.

The critical theorists call this kind of agenda a project of possibility (Simon 1987)—an activity that begins with a critique of *what is* but focuses primarily on *what could be*. These projects are the means through which we can sustain our sense of hope by working to change the social conditions that limit human potential. Since 1991, my projects of possibility have revolved around sustaining a form of whole language that is liberatory rather than confining, for both teachers and learners.

∿ Chapter Three

Expanding Whole Language

Facing Attacks

At the very time I want to argue for an expanded version of whole language, I find myself in a context within which even our limited notions of whole language theory and practice are under attack. While I believe that we have not yet begun to explore the liberatory potential of our theories of learning, critics contend that current practices of literacy education need to be made more rigorous by a return to "the basics." The dramatic shift to the right politically across North America has brought demands for more outside control of teachers' work through standards documents, standardized testing, and a focus on measurable outcomes. While I think many individual teachers are still committed to creating environments based on whole language philosophy, many others had such a tenuous hold on the changes brought about in the 1980s that it was only too easy for them to slip back into familiar and comfortable practices in the 1990s—especially since those approaches seem to garner so much more favor with parents and the wider community.

The public discourse about literacy education has definitely changed in Nova Scotia and across Canada. Parental concerns about phonics, spelling, and grammar have led many districts to put a renewed focus on those aspects of literacy. I certainly believe that there is a need to clarify how and when it is appropriate and useful to help children become aware of sounds, letters, word patterns, and other conventions of written language, but I see instead a rather alarming return to skills lessons that look very much like what we decided were not very productive forms of instruction fifteen years ago. Instead of addressing the existing confusions about the role that children's knowledge of language plays in their becoming effective language users, many constituencies have chosen to buy phonics workbooks, spelling programs, and software to teach the rules of grammar. Instead of creating new forms of staff development that engage teachers as learners and that help them to understand how to teach language and literacy from a whole language perspective, districts have bought into expensive and resource-hungry intervention programs. Instead of analyzing the systemic problems that hinder teachers' ability to meet the needs of their students (e.g. inflexible structures within schools, large classes, and teacher isolation), critics blame the teachers. Instead of analyzing the social and economic factors that often disempower students (e.g. poverty, race, and cultural differences), many blame the children.

Spelling, phonics, and grammar are easy targets for critics, especially since it is clear that many teachers did not have opportunities to learn how to embed these in whole language teaching. In my district, many children did "fall through the cracks" to arrive in the upper elementary grades without the strategies and skills they needed to revise, edit, and proofread their writing. We have seen many young children struggle unnecessarily with print because there was not enough direct attention in their classrooms to the grapho-phonic system. With a commitment to sustaining whole language philosophy, however, districts, schools, and teachers could address these difficulties relatively easily, especially since there are so many useful teacher resources now available to assist teachers in this area (see, for example, Cunningham and Cunningham 1992; Mills, O'Keefe, and Stephens, 1992; Rhodes and Dudley-Marling 1988; Phenix and Scott-Dunne 1991; Phenix 1995; Routman 1991; Scott 1993; Wilde 1992).

While the focus of critics has been on the perceived lack of attention to skills, this really masks a broader concern among both teachers and the community about the notion of teachers sharing power and control with their students. Phonics lessons, spelling tests, and basal readers are safe; they vest the control clearly outside the learner, in many cases not even with the teacher, but with the published program. A forced return to these guarantees that the larger agenda of whole language will be set aside. I believe we need to devote time and resources to shoring up the weak areas in order to make it possible for us to move forward to the larger issues, but it would be foolish to think that the critics will go away—even if we somehow prove the efficacy of our approaches in helping children learn to read and write.

If we are to move forward to the larger issues associated with expanding whole language, we must develop the will and the energy to carry out this task. We must learn to use the language of critique to make sense of our own experiences. We need to acknowledge that the "nice" versions of whole language, in which teachers concern themselves only with literacy as process, do not challenge the status quo because they are so easily incorporated into the way schools are supposed to be—into the dominant discourse of schooling. And, as we proceed, we need to recognize the wider implications of our whole language beliefs.

Rethinking the Roles of Teachers

While I believe that teachers must bring a more critical stance to their teaching, I am convinced that there is equally significant political work to be done outside the classroom. Although many teachers have told me they would prefer just to close the classroom door and work with their students, it is naive to think that critical classrooms can sustain themselves in happy isolation. The nature of the questions asked and the projects undertaken guarantees that this kind of teaching is a risky and public business. We know from our early experiences with whole language that even our less overtly political challenges to the status quo did not sit easily within the hierarchical school system. Those of us who have moved outside the classroom to positions of responsibility within that hierarchy cannot avoid taking on those bigger political issues, but I believe that we *all* need to make institutional structures, practices, and relationships the focus of our critique and projects of possibility. We all need to see ourselves both as teachers and as leaders engaged in social change.

We also need to make public the tensions and contradictions of this kind of teaching and leading, whether it is in a classroom, in a school, in a school district, or in the community outside the school system. The "nice" versions of whole language make teaching seem unproblematic. In these versions the major challenge is to find the right activity, to ask the right questions, or to use the most effective method—as if there could ever be these kinds of right answers to anything as complex as teaching.

When we become more explicitly political, we also make our beliefs and values much more public. Any of us who hold power in the institution (teachers in their classrooms, principals in their schools, central office staff in their districts) need to think about how that positions us in relationship to those with less power. I grapple continually with how to promote an agenda of social justice without limiting the freedom of those who hold other views. In working with teachers, it is extremely difficult to resist the temptation to use the power of my position to simply tell them how to teach, especially when I encounter practices that violate everything I believe about learning. Creating democratic learning environments is difficult work, whether the context is the individual classroom or a whole school district.

Field and Jardine (1994) artfully expose the tensions and contradictions inherent in this work through an interesting and useful analysis of what they term "bad examples" of whole language, for instance situations in which teachers have taken the whole language ownership message so seriously that they have left writing and reading almost totally in the hands of the children. These authors point out that in such a case, there is a very real danger of addressing the obvious need for a more active teacher role by re-establishing coercive power relationships. They also recognize that characterizing either extreme as an incomplete understanding of whole language would imply that there is a *complete* understanding somewhere —a whole language "final right answer" that will resolve forever the question of how to handle these power relationships in democratic classrooms. As the authors note:

> It is clear that whole language is not merely a shift in our language arts theories and practices. It is caught up in a nest of profound political, ethical, spiritual, and ecological orientations of our lives. It contains powerful notions: democratization, empowerment, ownership, choice, child-centeredness, authorship, silencing/ voice, images of being private, self-evaluation and self-expression, community and individuality. Given such an array, it is clear that the practice of whole language is a dangerous, risk-laden affair, full of implications and unforeseen consequences. We contend that these risks and dangers do not arise simply "from outside" but are part and parcel of whole language *itself*. The risks and potential dangers involved in handing over responsibility for writing to a group of 8-year-old children are not problems to be fixed. They are signs of the vitality and reality of the work we are doing. Even in the best examples of whole language theory and practice, these risks and dangers persist and require our interpretive caution and care. (259)

I have discovered no recipes or foolproof methods for how best to navigate the hazardous waters of our current economic, social, and political context or for how to deal with the many different kinds of tensions and contradictions we must face. I do know, however, that choosing to become more overtly political in my work has restored some of the sense of excitement and possibility with which I began my career. Despite the many constraints under which we all labor, it *is* possible to take action in ways that have the potential to make a difference in our own lives and those of our students.

⋀⋀⋀ *Chapter Four*

Moving Beyond "Whole Language Dress-up"

The Hole in Whole Language

In the many conversations I have had over the past five or six years about "what's wrong with whole language," critics usually get around to the contention that whole language is fine for children who learn easily and who come with the background knowledge they need to move immediately into print, but that it is not appropriate for readers and writers who struggle. This reasoning stems from an assumption that teachers who work from a whole language perspective do not believe in intervention but just let the learning unfold naturally, so children who need a greater degree of support will not be successful in whole language classrooms. Those who present this kind of argument usually then proceed to offer examples of children for whom this was true and for whom a heavy dose of phonics or some other form of intervention was the cure. This issue of "children falling through the cracks" or what some call "the hole in whole language" is pervasive. From what I have observed in my own district and from what I have learned from colleagues working in other areas of Canada and the United States, I believe we *should* be concerned about the literacy learning of many of our children. My concern, however, is not that whole language theory is lacking, but that many children are not learning to read and write because of the way that theory has been enacted in practice.

For some time I thought that the problems we were experiencing stemmed primarily from situations in which teachers did not have sufficient theoretical background to support their efforts in the classroom. That certainly accounts for some of our difficulties, but a critical incident a few years ago led me to believe that the issue is far more complex (Church 1994). In brief, several colleagues and I were leading a group of workshop participants through a series of activities to illustrate how to address "skills" within a literature-based program. I showed a videotape of a reading conference in which the teacher engaged actively with a student, challenging him to solve his own problems and to use the strategies she knew he had in his repertoire. Many participants objected to the directive way in which the teacher dealt with the student, despite the evidence that the child appeared relaxed and in the end quite pleased with his accomplishments. One woman commented, "I thought whole language was supposed to be warm and fuzzy!" It became obvious in the subsequent conversation that many in the audience believed that the teacher had interfered with the student's learning and pressured him too much. They saw her intervention as taking control away from the student and imposing a teacher agenda. Overall, they felt that the instruction demonstrated on the videotape was not consistent with their understanding of whole language philosophy.

I wish there had been time in that situation to talk at greater length with those teachers about how they view their roles in the classroom, because it seems to me our dialogue, while on the surface about skills, was really about one of the fundamental theoretical and practical tensions associated with whole language teaching: How are we to deal with issues of power and control in the classroom? While that is partly a pedagogical question, it is also a political question—a political question that does not have a "right answer." The question is integral to our struggles to create democratic classrooms and to enact curriculum derived from critical whole language theory. It underlies many of our debates about intervention, student choice, ownership, and critical literacy. To couch these issues in terms of a debate about what is the *real* whole language answer to how directly teachers should intervene not only oversimplifies the complexities of our work, but it also cuts off productive avenues of growth that we could pursue if we abandoned the search for right answers. For example, by virtue of my role as a teacher, I can never work without some kind of agenda. The question should not be about whether we pursue my agenda or the students' in the classroom, but about how we continually negotiate those agendas in ways that result in student learning. How do I encourage students to own their own writing and to develop their own voices and at the same time help them to expand their repertoire of writing styles and control of conventions? How do I raise questions that challenge children to think critically about texts without telling them what to think? How and when do I offer additional support to struggling readers and writers in ways that build and sustain their sense of themselves as successful learners? When do learning differences become learning difficulties? How broadly do I define literacy and literate behavior in order to accommodate the diverse learners I find in my classroom?

These questions and many more are ones to which we will, at best, find only temporary answers within particular contexts. Professional growth will not occur through our settling on those answers but through continually reflecting on the questions and, through that reflection, generating new questions. I can see this process at work in the development of my own belief system. For example, today I have a different view than I did ten years ago regarding how public we should make students' unedited writing. By encouraging children to display their early drafts or to send letters that had not been edited, we conveyed the wrong message to the students and to the community. We did not make sufficient distinction between writing that was in a form to be shared, and perhaps celebrated, within the classroom with peers and the teacher, and writing that was sufficiently polished to become public. We left many children with the impression that the content was all that was important, and we created great community anxiety about children's knowledge of spelling and other conventions. In an effort to allow children to own their writing and to avoid undue teacher interference in the process, many teachers did not assist children who were not yet able to edit their own writing. Yet changing my view on this issue does not mean I have no more questions. I still have to think about when and how writing should be made public and even what it means to be public: Is the classroom bulletin board public? How about a child's note to a parent? I have to think about how much self-editing I should expect from each student and how much help to provide. I need to consider how to offer assistance without taking over the writing. I need to judge when it is time to encourage a writer to come to closure on a piece and move on, and when more revision and editing will be helpful to the writing and the writer.

Because we were supposed to have finished our implementation of whole language a number of years ago, I have had few opportunities to share my rethinking on this issue and many others with the majority of teachers. They, in turn, have had little opportunity to share their questions and doubts. We seem to be stuck with whatever people thought whole language was five, and even ten, years ago. It is those versions of whole language, with the right answers they provided at the time, that spawned many of the myths and misconceptions that continue to plague us. I am quite willing to accept responsibility for giving teachers, students, and parents the impression that language conventions were not important; it is clear that something about the ways in which we talked about writing and dealt with the writing process in the early days did create that widespread belief. As well, my analysis of the history of whole language in Nova Scotia, outlined in Chapter Two, shows that the ways we structured learning for the teachers resulted in a focus on methodology. The way to move forward from here, I believe, is to learn from these past experiences. We should resist the temptation to create clearer definitions or to provide more up-to-date right answers about how to "do" whole language. Rather, all of us who are committed to sustaining whole language philosophy need to build on our current best theories of learning by inquiring into our uncertainties and questions.

Focusing on the Child

Instead of creating opportunites for classroom teachers to engage in professional inquiry, many districts and schools are devoting much collective energy and many resources to intervention programs that place the focus on remediating children outside the classroom. Consequently, they treat the literacy learning difficulties that many believe have been caused by whole language by focusing on the child instead of by helping classroom teachers to rethink their theories and practices.

Many of these programs are aimed at children in the early grades and report varying degrees of success as measured by standardized tests (Pikulski 1994). I am the most familiar with Reading Recovery, a program developed in New Zealand by Marie Clay, because it has been so widely implemented across Canada and the United States. Through this program, children potentially at risk for reading difficulties are identified at age six and receive intensive daily one-to-one instruction for twenty weeks. The program is designed to help children become more strategic readers and writers. Teachers who implement the Reading Recovery approach to remediation must receive a full year's training by a recognized Reading Recovery trainer. These trainers, in turn, must have participated in a full-year course at a certified Reading Recovery Training Site.

I have not joined in the enthusiasm expressed by colleagues who have received training and who are strong proponents of this approach. Advocates draw upon an impressive array of pre- and post-test data to demonstrate the efficacy of the program (Pinnell, Fried, and Eustice 1991). Anecdotal evidence is also positive; I know classroom and resource teachers who report noticeable improvements in children's ability to cope with reading and writing tasks. In addition to the direct benefits to the children, the training program does provide teachers with insights regarding literacy development. The year-long course involves teachers in looking carefully at how children make sense of print and at how the teacher's choice of materials and interventions influences that development. Teachers learn observation and assessment skills that certainly can be applied in other contexts. The training seems to address a need that many teachers I know have acknowledged: they really do not know very much about how children learn to read.

Why then, when this program appears to have so many benefits, do I have so many concerns about it? First, I have some serious philosophical difficulties with identifying children at age six as needing "recovery." Dyson (1994) and others caution us against leaping too quickly to the conclusion that children are "at risk." It may, in fact, be our own inability to respond to children's unique and individual ways of making sense of the world that is the prime contributor to children's learning difficulties. Programs like Reading Recovery vest the problem in the child, rather than in our failure to create classroom curriculum to support children's diverse needs. Dombey (1992) raises a similar concern: "[Reading Recovery] takes no account of the children's social, cultural, or linguistic conditions, nor of the experiences of other literacies which they may bring to school which have a crucial shaping influence on their learning" (5).

A second problem, which is related to the first, is that training teachers to deliver Reading Recovery does nothing to change the classroom program children are experiencing. Teachers may, in fact, gain insights that would make them more effective in the classroom, but the training is specifically designed to prepare them to carry out the one-to-one remediation outside the classroom. Short (1991) suggests that the classroom is the ideal place in which to become a more strategic reader and writer, since, as whole language theory suggests, literacy is best learned in a supportive social environment in which children learn from peers as well as the teacher. If all our classrooms provided these kinds of contexts, I wonder how many fewer children we would identify as "at risk" and in need of one-to-one remediation.

Third, the program defines literacy very narrowly. Its efficacy is measured through children's performance on standardized tests that tap into a limited set of skills that bear little relationship to reading and writing in authentic contexts. Dombey (1992) offers a further critique: "It is based on a narrow conception of reading, giving the child little help with developing larger text meanings or deeper understandings that inform the reading of skilled and committed young readers . . . its measures of success deal solely with word identification, ignoring even the literal meanings of the texts read" (6).

Fourth, knowing what I do about the complexities of literacy learning, I am resistant to what appear to be quick fixes and foolproof solutions. I realize that the leaders of the Reading Recovery movement do not intentionally present the program in that light, but followers seem to have rather a messianic fervor that gives me cause for concern. I know how quickly educational bureaucracies are to buy into approaches that appear to be the answer to pressing problems, especially when those programs have been marketed as successfully as Reading Recovery has across North America. I also know how quickly those answers can turn into new problems. For example, I would be very concerned to see districts devote most of their limited resources to training Reading Recovery teachers and thus ignore the professional development needs of classroom teachers. As I write, the provincial government in Nova Scotia has announced that it will allocate two hundred and fifty thousand dollars to train five Reading Recovery teacher-trainers— at a time when many districts are having difficulty scraping together funds for even modest professional development activities for classroom teachers.

As Curt Dudley-Marling (1994) has suggested, the real danger of Reading Recovery lies in its success. Because the program does seem to help children on their way to becoming readers and writers, it lets the institution off the hook. It allows us to continue to blame the children for their failures, rather than to address the systemic inequities based on gender, race, class, and culture that continue to disenfranchise large groups of students. It causes no change in the institutional practices that privilege white, middle-class students. It does not engage teachers and administrators in reflecting on how the culture and structures of schooling disempower both teachers and learners. It defines literacy learning as an issue of individual achievement rather than as a complex of social practices. Dudley-Marling argues, "Acknowledging literacy as social practice, however, enables us to challenge school discourse practices on ideological grounds. It enables us to see students not as illiterate, but as differently literate, not as deprived of literacy experiences, but possessing different literacy experiences" (9).

To me, Reading Recovery looks like another right answer, one that many seem to see as a solution to the problems created by whole language. It is a very compelling right answer because it comes with quantitative data to prove its worth (although questions are now being raised about its long-term efficacy and cost-effectiveness [Hiebert 1994]). It also has a growing army of trained teachers to help it prosper. It appeals to school systems that are under pressure to improve literacy learning; there is no doubt that rising standardized test scores can garner much praise. To truly meet the needs of our least successful literacy learners, however, I think we need to resist the lure of programs like this and to recast the problem as Dudley-Marling suggests. We also need to learn to explore ways to avoid perpetuating remedial cases by orchestrating the supports children need within the classroom.

For the same amount of money being spent on Reading Recovery and other similar programs, we could buy a great deal of professional development for classroom teachers. We could create learning contexts supportive to ongoing teacher growth and explore new ways of organizing classrooms and schools to make them more responsive to the diverse needs of their learners. We could generate and sustain ongoing conversations about how to negotiate power and control in the classroom so that children have time and space to develop in their own ways, but also receive the direct teacher support they need.

In the following section, I will describe a classroom in which a classroom teacher and a resource teacher work in collaboration to support all children. I present this not as a "right answer" for how to "do" whole language in the mid- to late-1990s, but as an example of teachers who continually raise new questions and reinvent their theories and practices. Both Linda Cook, the classroom teacher, and Florence MacLean-Kanary, the resource teacher, put issues of social justice at the center of their work—as a focus of the curriculum and as a guiding principle of life within the classroom. They are among a group of teachers whom I highly respect for their commitment and skill in valuing and responding to the diversity among their students. Every day in the classroom they provide powerful evidence to counteract the argument that whole language is only for middle-class children who learn easily.

Helping Children Learn to Read the World

When I asked Linda Cook to reflect on where she is with whole language now, she began by sharing the following observation:

> The children who come to me in grade four know all the jargon. They can tell me all about conferencing, reading journals, and the authoring cycle. During independent reading, they will pick up a book and look like they are reading. They know what to do

to convince you that they are reading and writing. They have figured out what is expected of them. But in many cases what they are doing has nothing at all to do with reading and writing. It is like they have mastered the surface features but not the substance of whole language.

Linda recalled her own first attempts to put new ideas into practice after returning from graduate study completed during a sabbatical leave seven or eight years ago. She began by developing a reading/writing workshop based on the work of Atwell (1987) and others, but she has continued to make revisions.

She notes:

I have worked to move beyond the pat, formulaic reading/writing workshop, which as I said earlier, can easily become simply another game of school for the children. The reading and writing does not seem to come out of a genuine need on the part of the students. I think many teachers have bought into the veneer: they publish books and have authors' teas, but it is often just a matter of looking like they are doing the right thing. I don't really blame the teachers. I would not be able to work the way I do had I not had a sabbatical leave. As well, there is a great deal of pressure for product, so published books and authors' teas demonstrate to administrators and parents that something is happening in the classroom. I wonder, however, how much is really happening, if the students I work with are an example. What I try to do is to create an environment in which reading and writing become important to the children because literacy has something to do with their lives—they are not just going through the motions any more. Of course, like other teachers, I have to deal with the constraints of parental and administrative expectations. I know I have to demonstrate publicly that the children are learning to read and write, so I try to strike a balance. But since I believe that exploratory talk, reading, and writing are central to children's development as readers and writers, I sometimes begrudge the time spent in more public displays of the children's learning. If I don't do these things, however, I know I won't be successful because I will spend all my time dealing with parental concerns.

Many of the elements of the reading/writing workshop are still evident in Linda's classroom. She provides a wide variety of reading materials and encourages extensive independent reading. The children also read in small groups, and they respond to their reading through journals, the visual arts, and drama. Linda guides children through a process as they write, and she helps them learn to draft, revise, edit, and proofread. The shift is not so much in *what* she does but *how* she does it. Several years ago, she might have viewed reading aloud to students as a relatively small part of her literacy program; she now devotes extensive time to this activity. She also spends more time leading large group discussions related to books she shares with the entire class. She believes that she must play an active role in guiding the children's discussion about the reading if they are to learn how to read and to talk about books. Linda poses questions that encourage the children to connect books with their lives, and she shares her own responses. She takes the time to pursue ideas and questions that seem to engage the children, moving beyond the text and back into it.

Throughout the day the classroom is alive with oral story-telling, stories that arise from the children's responses to their reading and stories that emerge as part of the ongoing classroom conversations. Linda believes that these conversations are essential to the children's development as readers and writers. Often children's writing topics evolve from the storytelling and other talk. While Linda has always had a strong writing program in her classroom, she believes devoting more time to talk—including discussions to help students draw connections between the books they are reading and writing topics they might choose—has been an important development in her approach. The attention to conversation has slowed the production of writing somewhat, but when the children do write, the process is much less of a struggle. Even the least able writers seem to believe they have something they want to say and are more willing to make the effort to say it.

Linda's version of whole language has always had a critical edge. A particular strength is her ability to weave the critical questions into the life of the classroom. She encourages children to question everything in order to understand what the world is about. One of the central questions is, What's important here? She recalls how Jerry Harste once spoke at a conference and talked about how children need to dig beneath the surface to consider, What's *really* going on here? She helps children understand that notion by comparing it to a classroom situation. As an example, she describes how a teacher might come into a room, find several children laughing in the corner, and ask, "What's going on?" The children might reply that they were just joking around, to which the teacher would dig deeper by responding, "What's *really* going on here?"

Linda's teaching embodies what Freire has called "reading the world" (Freire and Macedo 1987). In his view, becoming literate is a process through which learners come to understand the world by acting upon it through talk, reading, and writing. The stories and conversations that are at the heart of the curriculum are the means through which the children in Linda's classroom make sense of their world, as she guides them on this journey with her questions, comments, and invitations throughout the day.

Sometimes Linda's efforts to empower children to tell their own stories and to think for themselves run counter to parents' beliefs about schooling and about the world. In one experience, a child chose to pursue a classroom project despite her father's disapproval (Cook 1992). Having read *From Anna* (Little 1972), a book about a Jewish family's emigration to Canada during World War II, Linda's student Heather became fascinated by the issues surrounding the persecution of Jewish people during the war. When Linda asked each student to choose a topic from their novel as a focus for a research project, this young girl decided to undertake a study of Israel. Shortly after making this decision, Heather confided to Linda that her father did not want her to explore that topic because he "just didn't like those people." Despite Linda's suggestion that the student choose a different topic, the child was determined to pursue her original idea. After further discussion, in which it became obvious that Heather had a compelling interest to learn more about the history surrounding the novel she had found so engaging, Linda decided not to intervene and allowed the study to unfold. With this decision, Linda faced a moral and ethical dilemma as she was caught between her desire to empower the child to direct her own learning and her concern about the possible consequences should the parent decide to take action against his daughter or her teacher. This incident influenced Linda to explore new ways to involve parents in their children's learning and in the life of the classroom. She is not prepared to back away from her agenda of empowerment, but she also recognizes the need to empower parents through dialogue and participation:

> It takes continual dialogue and demonstration to allay fears of failure that keep parents on edge with me, the person they see as being 'in charge.' It means holding conversations in nonthreatening settings, with each side appreciating what the other has to say. I continue to invite parents to participate in classroom enterprises, to be active participants in their children's learning. I try to keep in mind the importance of sharing control with one's students in the classroom and with their parents beyond it. (Cook 1992, 291)

Linda's classroom clearly is a place in which all participants, both adults and children, have value. Of all the teachers I know, Linda is among the most gifted in meeting the needs of a diverse range of learners. Part of what motivated her to allow the project on Israel to unfold was her knowledge of Heather's previous learning difficulties. Linda recognized that this particular inquiry would be a powerful means through which Heather could grow in skill and confidence as a learner by finding answers to questions that puzzled and intrigued her. Unlike the critics of whole language teaching who suggest that the way to "fix" students' problems is through greater attention to skills or through remedial programs like Reading Recovery, Linda believes that children's needs can be met within a classroom in which the teacher expects all children to learn and provides the support that is needed so they *can* learn.

How does Linda actually make it possible for so many diverse learners to be successful? As the school district has moved toward the inclusion of all children in regular classrooms, she has seen an increase in the range and severity of the learning difficulties experienced by her students. Side by side with the children who struggle with reading and writing and those who have only a surface understanding of reading and writing processes are others whose physical and mental challenges significantly affect their ability to learn. In meeting the needs of these children and those in her classroom who learn more easily, Linda begins by actively resisting conventional notions about what is possible. She thinks of children as having different learning styles rather than as having learning difficulties. She believes that all children have strengths and important and interesting stories to tell. She makes the differences among the children a frequent topic of conversation within the classroom. As she puts it,

> The children know that some of them learn more easily and quickly than others. There is no point in trying to hide it, so I point out the differences, such as they will learn at different rates and in different ways, and everyone has difficulties to overcome. I don't treat the children with learning problems as lepers by setting them apart from the others. When the emphasis is on the differences among all the children, those with significant learning difficulties become part of the overall diversity of the group, not anomalies.

Linda also expects all the children to engage with the curriculum in whatever ways they can. All children make contributions to the frequent conversations that shape the day in the classroom. Everyone's stories count. During the large blocks of time devoted to reading and writing, all children participate. There is no choice about whether or not to engage, but there are many choices about reading materials and writing topics. Linda's classroom is very unlike those mythical whole language classrooms in which learning is supposed to unfold naturally. As she describes it,

> I am really quite directive, I guess. The classroom is tightly structured, and I set clear expectations. I try to set children up for success by offering them the information and support they need to be successful. What I do is a product of what I have learned by working with children over the years, but it continually changes as I incorporate new perspectives from professional reading, conferences, and talking with other teachers. Since my sabbatical year, I have taken every opportunity I could to continue to learn. It seems as if I draw a bit from all of the conversations, courses, and books I have read. I was quite upset some time ago when I lost the notebook in which I had been jotting down ideas, thoughts, and perspectives from all those sources over several years, but I discovered that it was still all in my head. It seems to be a continual process of adding to what I know.

Orchestrating Classroom Supports

Linda attributes her recent success in meeting the diverse needs of children to her collaboration with Florence, who supports children *within* the classroom rather than withdrawing them for one-to-one or small group assistance. Like Linda, Florence completed a graduate program in literacy education at Mount Saint Vincent several years ago. Before moving into her present support role, she was an extremely effective classroom teacher, and she brings that experience to her work with other teachers. She also worked in the private sector for two years, applying whole language principles to career development programs with unemployed adults. Because she has orchestrated the many facets of classroom teaching herself,

Florence not only has credibility in her support role, but she also is able to respond quickly and spontaneously as children's needs arise.

Florence's beliefs about her role are grounded in a strong philosophy of social justice and equity:

> Children with learning difficulties belong in the classroom. They have to remain in a place of dignity, not drawn away from the social environment to be taught in isolation. I could not do what I do with the children in a traditional remedial setting. Working in the classroom allows me to maximize on the children's strengths. Here they have many opportunities to express themselves and to be part of the classroom conversations. They learn a great deal from the other children. I have been working with one child this year who had been withdrawn from the classroom so much that he had no idea how to function in the group. The reports from his previous teacher said, "he won't do anything in the classroom." We made it a goal early in the year to change that, and through coaching from both of us and from peers, he made great strides. Early in the year he often held his head down and seemed unwilling or unable to respond either orally or in writing. We set clear expectations that he must participate and then structured many positive experiences, primarily in the context of mathematics. I worked with him on problem-solving, engaging him in daily math talk and interaction with peers. He learned how to use the language of math, and by the end of the year he could function quite successfully with the class, both academically and socially. That would never have happened if I had continued to withdraw him.

Linda and Florence recognize that often both classroom and support teachers favor the withdrawing of students from the classroom for specific interventions. They believe that this only serves to further disconnect these learners from the ongoing life of the classroom, often exacerbating the difficulties they are experiencing. The gaps between these students and their peers continually widen because they have not received meaningful interventions within a classroom environment in which teachers expect that they can learn. Because the two women have very similar beliefs about learning and teaching, they have developed effective ways of supporting all the children. While Florence pays specific attention to children with learning difficulties, she is a resource to the entire classroom. The children see her as a co-teacher with Linda, not the remedial teacher who deals only with those who are not successful.

There is, however, a clear structure and purpose to Florence's work with the students who are struggling. She and Linda develop a plan for how they will support each child, and together they consult with parents and other professionals such as speech language pathologists and psychologists as the year evolves. During the time Linda sets aside for independent reading and writing, Florence often focuses on the needs of small groups of children. For example, during the 1994–95 school year, there were four or five children in Linda's classroom who barely were able to cope with the simplest reading material. One child had come from a special education setting in which she had learned to decode beautifully, but had no idea what she was reading. Another was quite bright, but had a significant learning disability that had impeded his literacy learning. Others had developmental delays and were just beginning to make sense of written language. All the children were functioning well below the level of most of their peers and had struggled with learning since entering school.

Florence arranged to be in Linda's classroom on a regular schedule for an hour each day, and the two teachers began an intensive program to address the children's individual needs. At the same time that this individual and small group work was occurring, Linda continued to involve the students in all the experiences she planned for the whole class. Wherever possible, Florence built her interactions around those experiences, such as fostering the children's further exploration of topics that arose in the classroom discussions. To help the children who were struggling to gain confidence and fluency, the teachers knew that they had to provide reading material that the children could handle. All the children in the classroom had opportunities to choose books for independent and small group readings, so the teachers gathered multiple copies of simple "chapter books" to add to the classroom library. They chose a series that revolved around the adventures of a team of characters that they thought the children would find engaging. At first, the children who were struggling were reluctant to read these books, but the two teachers worked together to make the children's reading experiences positive and purposeful. Both were honest and open with the children, discussing with each of them the difficulties they were experiencing and the ways that reading the chapter books might help them. Florence then worked with the children individually and in a group, helping them not only to develop specific strategies, but also to build confidence in their own abilities. She talked with the children about whether they really wanted to learn to read and assured them that if they did, she knew how to help them. The children read in their small group and individually, and they learned how to help each other. Both teachers emphasized the flexible use of reading strategies and immersed the children in language. They engaged the children in frequent word play and discussions that connected learning to the classroom and to the children's lives outside school. The teachers involved parents in daily reading with the children at home.

Although there was an emphasis on reading instruction, Florence provided support in other contexts, as well. For example, she frequently held writing conferences with children to assist them in generating and organizing their ideas. She helped them create word webs and then to expand these through discussion and exploratory writing. She found that this kind of intense interaction enabled children to tap into background experiences and knowledge they did not know they had. Some of the children were also struggling with mathematics, especially with problem-solving. To them, math was the rote performance of computations, and they did not know how to deal with more complex problems. They struggled with the language of math problems and were at a loss when confronted with specialized terminology. Using a variety of math manipulatives as a support, Florence guided the children through these problems, focusing them through her questions: What are the cue words (*altogether, total, difference*) in the problem? What are you asked to do in this problem? Can you show me how to do it? Once the children became more confident with the language of math and the application of math concepts, the teachers invited the children to create their own problems by applying what they had learned to real life experiences. For example, the children might create problems around photographs or illustrations from magazines. To do this, they needed to determine what information was needed, to translate that information into mathematical language, to decide what question to ask, and then to check to see if the problem was solvable. In Florence's words, "This whole process is indeed a stretch to higher learning levels for the children—a real challenge!"

The teachers set the children up for success, making reasonable requests within the classroom environment. They were flexible in their expectations: if novel reading could not happen at home because of math homework, then the math page became the reading lesson. The intervention was quite direct. As Linda described it, "When children encounter problems, Florence is not afraid to give them information. She offers them specific help with how to make their way through text. She tells them, 'this is how you do it, and here are some things you should look for.'"

Children's parents were active partners in this process. The teachers communicated frequently with parents and showed them how to help the children at home, encouraging them to see support for literacy as broadly as possible. For example, they suggested how parents could use magazines, newspapers, shopping lists, and other functional texts to make reading and writing a part of daily life. Many parents expressed great relief when they heard that their children would not be withdrawn for remediation. They described the children's feelings of isolation and failure as a result of years of this kind of intervention. By the end of the year, the children all had made considerable progress. Academically, most were functioning comfortably with their peers. They were visibly more confident and showed a new eagerness to come to school. Because the children had gained so much during the year, the teachers suggested to the administration that Linda move on with the students to the next year. In the fall of 1995, Linda and Florence picked up where they had left off with these students and with others in Linda's classroom.

In summary, many factors interact to make Linda's classroom such a supportive learning environment for diverse learners. Linda has high expectations and provides the support necessary for children to meet those expectations. She demonstrates clearly that she values individual differences and fosters all children's sense of belonging. She creates a supportive social environment in which the children help each other. She immerses the children in language, including all of them in the storytelling, conversations, and word play. Linda and Florence function as a highly coordinated and collaborative team, continually expressing their confidence in the children's ability to be successful. Linda talked with me about the significance of her collaboration with Florence:

> She helps to validate what I am doing. When I become discouraged, she points out the progress we are making. It is wonderful to have someone to think and talk with, as I struggle with the problems I encounter. I don't feel as if I am all alone in the classroom, totally responsible to meet all the needs on my own. But it only works because Florence and I work from a similar philosophy; it would be impossible to have this kind of collaboration if there were conflicting beliefs.

Both teachers work from a clearly articulated learning theory and engage in ongoing reflection about their work. Drawing upon her experiences as a classroom teacher, Florence orchestrates direct and focused attention to the children's individual needs within the classroom, judging when specific information about strategies and techniques will be helpful to individuals and groups. The teachers include parents and other professionals as active partners in the learning process.

It is the work of teachers like Linda and Florence that sustains my confidence in the power of whole language philosophy. It is in classrooms like Linda's that the promise of that philosophy comes the closest to being fulfilled. Teachers like these bring a truly critical perspective to their work, as they insist upon the rights of all children to participate fully in the classroom and to receive the instruction they need within that context. It is to these classrooms and teachers that I turn when I find myself questioning my own firmly held assumption that all children can learn within the regular classroom, given a knowledgeable teacher and appropriate supports, including resource teachers who know how to work effectively within the classroom. That assumption is challenged frequently, as many insist that classroom teachers cannot "do it all" and propose various kinds of support systems outside the classroom. I would never argue that classroom teachers can "do it all," but I believe we could transform classrooms if more teachers both understood whole language theory and enacted it skillfully and reflectively. We could explore different ways of providing support to increasingly diverse groups of learners through the kind of collaborative working relationships that Linda and Florence have developed. We could push the boundaries of the classroom to invite parents and other community members into the collaboration and to provide experiences in the community for all learners. We could break out of our classroom—and school building—boxes.

∿∿∿ Chapter Five

Cutting Teachers Some Slack

Supporting Teacher Growth

While I have always had an interest in the issues surrounding professional development, it was my experiences with the *Opening Our Doors* project that convinced me that we need to create radically different ways of supporting teacher growth. From my reflections on that incident, I concluded not only that traditional forms of staff development are not supportive of teacher change, but that well-intentioned efforts to create alternatives can easily be distorted and subverted. I learned how important it is to understand the institutional context within which these change efforts occur. The kind of learning environment I created for my committee clearly did support change among the actual participants. Committee members reflected that this professional development experience caused them to grow and change in unexpected ways. Our problems arose when we tried to move beyond that small group to invite others into the conversation. Our audience brought their own interpretations to the invitation—interpretations that were influenced by their prior experiences with top-down curriculum change within a hierarchical school system.

Although I was discouraged about the reactions of our audience and disappointed that the book project failed as a district-wide change initiative, I saw my work with the committee as a success. It provided evidence that it is possible to effect significant teacher change, given the right circumstances. I recognized the similarities among the committee and the networks and study groups that fostered the early growth of whole language in Nova Scotia. Both were power-ful learning contexts that, I believe, derived their strength from the leaders' and participants' understanding of whole language philosophy. That understanding enabled us to develop structures, relationships, attitudes, and procedures that fostered teachers' learning.

In both contexts teachers had choices; they voluntarily en-gaged in sustained professional conversations and collectively shaped the direction of the group's undertakings. In both in-stances we focused on making sense of our own experiences, grounding our inquiry in our work with students. We used language for learning by talking, reading, and writing about issues and questions that mattered to us. The group accepted and valued the diverse perspectives of all participants. We often fought our way to an understanding of complex issues, sometimes agreeing to disagree. We made ourselves vulnera-ble by sharing our questions, doubts, and uncertainties. There was a "lead teacher" in each situation: a person who took responsibility for calling meetings; for structuring the tasks when necessary; for keeping the group moving; for supporting individuals and small groups; and for facilitating the writing. As each group gained experience in working together, the lead teacher's role became less important; the group became much more self-directed with all members taking leadership in dif-ferent ways. All members shared a commitment to learning from each other. While the group shared common purposes and tasks, group members valued and celebrated individuals' differing interests, strengths, approaches, and perspectives. In short, both situations were very much like learning in an ef-fective whole language classroom.

I certainly have enough evidence to convince me that teachers need opportunities to learn in environments based upon whole language principles. I know that if we are to revisit literacy education in the ways I have suggested earlier in this book—to shore up the gains we have already made and to expand whole language to become more critical and overtly political—the key is in supporting the growth of teachers. Yet I find myself continually grappling with the political realities of making that possible in the hierarchical institution in which I work. Moreover, I have undertaken this project at a time when many teachers feel under siege both because they are the brunt of criticism from all sides and because their work has become increasingly complex, time-consuming, frustrating and bone-wearying. Since I left a school-based assignment eleven years ago, the factors influencing teachers' lives have been profound and often contradictory: severe fiscal restraints; an accelerated shift from an industrial-based to an information- and technology-based economy; the change in student populations to reflect much greater linguistic and cultural diversity; the inclusion of many more students with significant mental and physical challenges; societal changes that have created a growing population of "at risk" students; restructuring, strategic planning, and site-based management; and top-down curricular reform.

What further complicates attempts to refocus on literacy education in my district and across Nova Scotia is the widely held belief that whole language has been proven to be an ineffective model for literacy learning. I have heard many describe our present situation as an inevitable pendulum swing back to practices such as phonics instruction that worked in the past. I have seen my own efforts to engage teachers in conversations about the sound system of language or about spelling interpreted as a sign that "whole language is dead." While there are certainly many teachers in my district and in this province who have continued to grapple with the complexities of whole language teaching, I see much less attention and time devoted to literacy teaching and learning in school-based in-services and in other professional development activities. As recently as 1989, hundreds of teachers attended the annual provincial reading conference; now those who participate tend to be a much smaller group of committed educators. I suspect this lack of involvement is due to a combination of factors: less general support for teacher professional development from school systems and the province; the increasing demands and stresses on teachers; the pervasive resistance and cynicism that was a legacy of the provincial whole language implementation; and, for some, a belief that they have "finished" whole language and can now move on to science, math, or some other subject. Under these circumstances, I have felt I needed to approach this project with care and caution, keeping in mind the potential pitfalls. Having been through several failed experiments in teacher change, I am considerably wiser and more realistic about the difficulties inherent in this work.

The literature on educational change suggests we can never overstate the challenges of restructuring schools and school systems that are remarkably resistant to efforts to reform them (Fullan and Hargreaves 1991; Fullan 1993). Changes that do occur are frequently what Cuban (1988) termed "first order changes," which "make what already exists more efficient and more effective, without disturbing the basic organizational features, without substantially altering the ways in which adults and children perform their roles" (342). He contrasts these with "second order changes," which "seek to alter the fundamental ways in which organizations are put together . . . [and] transform familiar ways of doing things into new ways of solving persistent problems" (342). Whole language, conceptualized as a philosophy and a perspective on teaching and learning, is a second order change; whole language, actualized as a movement and a method for teaching reading and writing, has too often resulted in only first order changes. Given the complexity of the second order changes associated with whole language as a philosophy—the need to create collaborative, learning communities within schools that not only support the growth of children but also foster ongoing change and development among the professional staff who work there—it is not surprising that it is only the superficial aspects of whole language that have taken hold in many classrooms, schools, and school districts. These first order type changes seem to have been adopted relatively easily; for example, in many areas teachers have incorporated some form of reading/writing workshop in place of reading instruction organized through basal reading programs. It is much rarer to find classrooms, schools or districts that have been transformed through administrators' and teachers' ongoing efforts to enact whole language philosophy. As researchers like Fullan and Cuban suggest, schools and schools systems are resistant to these types of reform.

How, then, do we promote second order changes? In a thoughtful and penetrating inquiry into teachers' work and culture, Hargreaves (1994) examines many of the paradoxes associated with introducing concepts like collegiality, collaboration, and restructuring within hierarchical bureaucracies. In his view, most reforms have failed because they have not dealt with the most important influences on teachers' work:

> These are the teacher's *purpose*, which drives what the teacher does; the kind of *person* the teacher is, in their life as well as their work, and how this affects their teaching; the *context* in which teachers work, which limits or liberates them in terms of what they can achieve; and the *culture* of the teaching community and how teachers' relationships (or lack of them) with their colleagues can support or subvert them in their efforts to improve the quality of what they offer to their students. (xiv)

As I have moved on from my experiences with *Opening Our Doors*, my journey has been informed by the work of researchers like Hargreaves (Barth 1990; Brown 1991; Fullan and Hargreaves 1991; Fullan and Miles 1992; Riley 1992, Schlechty 1990; Senge 1990; Sergiovanni 1992; Sizer 1992; Tye 1992). I have tried to find ways to subvert the hierarchy by creating more open structures and relationships. I have thought a great deal about Trimbur's (1989) notion of consensus "not as agreement that reconciles differences through an ideal conversation but rather as the desire of humans to live and work together with differences" (246). I return to this quote again and again. It captures for me the fundamental problem with the way whole language was enacted as a set of correct practices imposed on teachers from above. Whether teachers agreed with the change or had a different perspective on teaching or learning was never on the table for discussion. Even the few opportunities for teachers to interact were too often examples of what Hargreaves (1994) terms "contrived collegiality," in which administrators structure what appear to be collaborative situations "to implement non-negotiable programs and curricula whose viability and practicality are not open to discussion" (80).

Reopening Conversations

Professional Dialogue

The professional development initiatives I am about to describe are extremely modest and exploratory. They represent my efforts to reopen the conversations about literacy education in the district as a first step in the larger project of revising and expanding whole language, and they include my attempts to apply some of the lessons I have learned about teacher change. Several years ago I began this undertaking by meeting with groups and individuals in the district who I knew had real concerns about the effects whole language teaching appeared to be having on children. I knew that many of the speech-language pathologists in the district and across the province increasingly viewed their role as patching up the problems created by whole language. They had seen an alarming increase in the number of referrals of children who did not seem to be making sense of print because they had no idea how to draw upon grapho-phonic information. As part of their work with these children, many of the speech-language pathologists were using an auditory training program designed to develop phonological awareness. As well, a group of their colleagues had established a very successful private clinic in which the same training program was being used extensively. Many of our resource teachers, too, seemed to be spending a great deal of time on activities that looked like phonics lessons in isolation as an effort to respond to the "hole in whole language."

Although I recognized the legitimacy of the problems these professionals had identified—a disproportionate number of children were struggling with reading and writing—I disagreed with their analysis of the problem and with their solutions. I believed we needed to help teachers understand more about the role of the grapho-phonic system in reading and writing, but not to blame whole language. More important, we needed to develop supports for students that were consistent with whole language instead of resorting to skills-based training programs or to phonics in isolation.

In a conscious effort to create more equal power relationships, I resisted the temptation to offer my solutions, to criticize what they were doing, or to ban the use of the training program. Instead, I asked them to help me understand what seemed to be happening to the children. That small change in approach made all the difference. I found myself having the kind of real conversations that are common in everyday life but rare in school systems, especially across levels of the hierarchy. We offered our different perspectives, argued our points of view, drew on different kinds of evidence to support our positions, and gradually began to see a great deal of common ground.

New Working Relationships

Through these meetings and informal one-to-one discussions, I forged strong and generative working relationships with several of the speech-language pathologists. It was enlightening to broaden my understanding of language/literacy development by tapping into their expertise and their professional literature. In turn, I was able to assist them in gaining more in-depth knowledge of literacy learning from a whole language perspective. We discovered that we all believed in the central role of meaning making in language learning; in the necessity for children to orchestrate all the language systems—pragmatics, semantics, syntax, and phonology—in order to become effective language users; and in the interrelatedness of oral and written language and other communication systems. Because of her particular interest in oral language literacy connections, I found myself talking at length with Lynne Healy, one of the speech language pathologists. In her work with children, Lynne moved away from the auditory training program she had been using. Instead, she developed more purposeful and meaningful ways to enhance children's knowledge of phonology, particularly through rhyming, and to help them become aware of the many different kinds of patterns in language. As Lynne and I reflected upon her experiences with the children, we concluded that some learners need a great deal more experience with rhyme than we typically include in early literacy programs. When Lynne provided the focused and meaningful work with sound patterns that these children seemed to need, they began to make progress as readers and writers. We also incorporated recent insights about helping children learn to spell that reflect a similar focus on patterns, not just those of sound, but of meaning and function (Phenix and Scott-Dunne 1991; Scott 1993).

Invitations to Schools

As time went by, we invited other speech-language pathologists, resource teachers, and classroom teachers into our conversation. We also extended an invitation to schools to consider using some of their inservice time to revisit literacy learning with us. Over the course of two years, five or six schools accepted this invitation, and Lynne and I led them through inservice experiences designed to help them generate and explore their own questions. To begin, we attended a half-day session with the staff to share some of the issues we had been attempting to address in our collaborative work. I made it a point to raise the topic of the history of whole language in the district as part of my introductory comments.

In most instances, my reflections on the implementation problems prompted teachers to offer their perspectives and to identify issues they wanted to address. Often these revolved around their confusion about how much and what kind of direct teacher support they ought to be offering children who were struggling with reading and writing. It was apparent that many of them were still angry and frustrated about the early whole language inservices and felt that the leaders of those sessions had not offered them a coherent and viable model for literacy learning. As a result, many of them had developed a rather eclectic mix of whole language practices and techniques such as phonics lessons and spelling lists.

By the end of these sessions, the groups usually had identified a series of issues and questions we could use to frame future workshops. In general, we found that teachers wanted and needed to learn more about how to develop knowledge of the sound system. We chose to address that need by leading them through a series of activities designed to help them see how all four language systems operate in oral and written language. In most cases, schools chose to devote two inservice days to these workshops. While we found that some teachers seemed to benefit greatly from these sessions, for most there was too much new information presented over too short a time frame. Although we tried to build in a process for teachers to attempt to apply what they were learning in the sessions to their work in the classroom and then to discuss the results, we were not very successful. Because of our other responsibilities we could not provide any ongoing support to the teachers between the sessions, so it is not surprising that they did not make many changes in their classrooms. In the school where Lynne was assigned as a speech-language pathologist, we saw more change because some teachers did invite her into the classroom to work with them as they incorporated new approaches. Moreover, she was available to teachers who wished to follow up on the sessions with questions or further discussion. Overall, however, while we felt we had certainly increased the teachers' awareness and perhaps broadened the knowledge base of some, we knew this approach to professional development was still too brief and fragmented to effect real change.

Long-term Staff Development

Probably Lynne and I learned more through these sessions than anyone else. We became clearer about what we believed and about what that meant for literacy teaching. We also learned not to make assumptions about teachers' prior knowledge; most of them did not know about the four language systems or about how to use such techniques as miscue analysis to gather information about children's reading. We eventually came to realize that we were asking the impossible of the teachers; they could not be expected to make sense of all this new knowledge about language development in the short time we had available. Therefore, we began to think about how we might create a longer and more in-depth experience for teachers. Around the same time, I discussed the problem with Judith Newman, who had taken a position as Dean of the Faculty of Education at the University of Manitoba. She told me about some work that Diane Stephens of the University of Hawaii was doing with teachers. Diane had been engaging the teachers in working one-on-one with children in situations in which she was available to give them feedback. Diane also provided these teachers with opportunities to talk with each other about what they were learning in these sessions. Judith herself was exploring the possibilities for a similar long-term staff development project with schools in Winnipeg. She suggested that I might try to do the same.

Creating New Learning Contexts

Several colleagues, including Lynne, expressed a great deal of interest in the idea. Through informal discussions with supervisory colleagues and school-based staff, I gathered a

steering committee comprised of two curriculum supervisors, two speech-language pathologists, and representatives
from three schools that expressed an interest in becoming
involved. One of the three original schools, a rural school
with only four teachers, invited a neighboring school to join
them to increase their team to seven. The second school had
five teachers involved, and the third had seven. Participants
were classroom teachers, primarily of grades two and three,
and resource teachers. I had some discretion in the use of
funds to hire substitutes for professional development activities, so I was able to assign the equivalent of one day of release time per month per teacher that the schools could use
in any way they wished. This release time proved to be one
of the most important ways in which I provided administrative support to this project. To engage in the kind of inquiry
that eventually led to changes in their beliefs and practices,
teachers needed time away from those classrooms during the
school day.

The steering committee guided the project throughout the
year. Members of this committee met a number of times to
discuss what was happening at each school and to shape
future directions. The entire project team met three times
during the year: at a summer institute held in August before
school opening, in December, and in March. All schools
worked from a common framework, but each developed an
individual plan for how to proceed at the school. Participants
agreed that each teacher would work with an individual child,
carrying out an informal assessment of the student's literacy
learning and developing appropriate instruction based upon
what they learned about the child. School teams would meet
regularly to share questions and insights about the children
whom they had selected and to explore the classroom implications of what they were learning. The group agreed upon
the following overall goal: To improve and enhance literacy
learning in the classroom by studying the learning experiences of one student over a school year. The following sub-
goals emerged from that:

1. To enhance teachers' knowledge of literacy learning, with an emphasis on providing appropriate instruction for "at risk" learners.
2. To explore ways in which Student Services' staff can be used more effectively to support teachers and children.
3. To create communities of inquiry that include teachers both within and outside the district.
4. To develop a staff development model that incorporates insights from the research literature related to educational change.
5. To explore ways in which supervisory staff and teacher-leaders can be used most effectively to support school-based staff development.

Each school carried the project out for nearly the whole school year. While there was growth and change in all three schools, one in particular demonstrated the power of this kind of model for staff development. A second had the potential for similar progress, but administrative and staff changes mid-year disrupted the project, so they did not move along quite as quickly. In the third, the teachers, while no less capable and committed than the others, were handicapped because of a lack of administrative support and involvement. That team had a great deal of difficulty sustaining the process without some form of leadership on-site. Two kinds of leadership seemed essential: overall recognition and valuing of the project within the school, which had to come from the principal; and facilitation of group meetings and the contribution of expertise to the group discussions, which did not have to come from an administrator, but needed administrative sanction.

In the school where change was most evident, the vice-principal played both leadership roles, supported by the principal in important ways. In the fall, when the project was just getting under way, members of the staff who were not directly involved attempted to subvert the initiative, largely through negative comments in the staff room but also through attempts to convince one of the participants to withdraw. The administrative team made it clear to the entire staff that such behavior was unacceptable. They also kept all other staff members continually informed about how the work was proceeding and what the teachers were learning. That openness seemed to prevent the development of camps and in-groups and out-groups, and it led other staff members to view the project in a positive light. As the year progressed, a number of other teachers expressed an interest in becoming involved during the next school year.

In this school in particular, the teachers moved beyond superficial discussions of practices to engage in professional inquiry. The vice-principal attributed that shift to the opportunities they had for sustained conversations at regularly scheduled times during the work day. He modestly underplayed his own role as a leader, but, from my perspective, it appears that his facilitation was central to the process. He helped the teachers to develop a workable structure and, especially in the early meetings, asked the probing questions that caused the teachers to question their assumptions. From the beginning, he worked to shift control of the agenda to the teachers themselves. Since they saw me as the overall initiator of the project, the teachers kept asking, What does Susan want? It was some time before they believed that they had the power to take the project where they wanted it to go, within the broad framework we had established. They seemed unwilling to trust that someone was actually "cutting them some slack," as they described it. They seemed equally reluctant, at first, to make public their questions and uncertainties. Over time, however, they became increasingly open and reflective. They began to express their honest opinions and feelings, not what they thought they were "supposed" to believe. They used the group as a sounding board when they felt stuck about where to go next with an individual child or the class as a whole. Sometimes discussions became so heated that individuals had to leave the room to cool off. One teacher offered the following final reflection:

> The extent to which I have grown both personally and professionally this year is directly related to the literacy project. In the history of my teaching career I don't ever remember experiences that have stretched my metacognitive abilities to the point of mental fatigue. Unquestionably, this paradigm of professional development needs to take place within our schools if change is really to be affected. Professional communities must be established within our schools in order to foster ongoing inquiry.

The three meetings of the entire project team were significant to all the teachers. They appreciated having the opportunity to move outside the closely knit school-based groups to test out their ideas and perceptions within a larger context. As leaders, the steering committee found these sessions invaluable for getting a sense of how the project was unfolding. We had hoped to broaden the conversation further through e-mail correspondence with Winnipeg and Hawaii, but that proved too ambitious, given the time and resources we had available. Although we had to settle for our local collaboration, we were all extremely impressed with the depth and breadth of the discussions. One of the teachers from the rural area commented that she had felt extremely intimidated at first, but had been relieved to discover that all the teachers shared similar anxieties and uncertainties. It was especially vital for the teachers from the outlying areas to make these kinds of connections with peers; too often, they work in relative isolation with, at most, three or four other colleagues with whom to interact. By March, when we held the final meeting, the teachers no longer wanted to meet in the safety of groups of two or three, but gathered as a whole group for a lengthy discussion of the implications of what they had learned from the project.

It was clear that they had discovered a great deal about literacy learning through working with an individual child.

Most of them had not used miscue analysis or running records before, and they indicated they had found these assessment tools enormously helpful and would continue to use them. Teachers found that most of the children did not have a broad repertoire of techniques and strategies for solving problems as they read. The children benefitted greatly from extensive reading of material with which they were comfortable, from focused discussion, from experiences with the visual arts, and from writing. The teachers talked about the need to involve parents in the process, especially to prevent situations in which home and school were working at cross-purposes. For example, a number of parents in one community had purchased a widely advertised phonics program and were drilling the children at home at the same time that the teachers were trying to move the children away from total reliance on the graphophonic system. The teachers talked about the many social issues that were influencing their children's lives and literacy development: poverty, in both rural and urban settings; conflict or violence in the home; parents holding two or three jobs to keep the family together; and so on. In at least one school, the discussion became more political as the teachers moved beyond a concern with cuing systems to analyze the many other factors that might cause a child to struggle with literacy or to have difficulty concentrating in class.

For those of us familiar with whole language theory and practices, there was nothing surprising in their discoveries. However, it was clear that the teachers had not acquired this essential information about literacy learning and teaching through preservice or inservice education. Since most of them were experienced teachers, we did not expect that their teacher education programs would have been based upon whole language theories. Yet, it was sobering for those of us who led the project to see the obvious inadequacies of the inservice education the teachers had received. If these talented, intelligent, and skilled teachers had clearly had so many gaps in their understanding, where did that leave the majority of teachers across the district? We were encouraged, however, to see the growth that occurred in many of these teachers, as well as their strong desire to keep on learning.

While the teachers were intrigued by what they were learning about the children, their real excitement and enthusiasm stemmed from their own experiences as learners. Even the teachers who lacked administrative support felt they had learned from working with each other. In one school, the classroom and resource teachers involved in the project developed more effective ways of working together in the classroom to support children with difficulties. They built a much broader shared understanding of goals and processes and thus were able to collaborate, rather than simply to work side by side. Sometimes the roles reversed, and a resource teacher took the whole class to allow the classroom teacher to work with individuals or small groups. One resource teacher commented that in the past she often felt like a glorified teacher's aide when she tried to work in the classroom—both because she and the teachers were often working from different assumptions, but also because they had so little opportunity for discussion and planning. Here again, administrators provided support by scheduling common planning time for the teachers in addition to the time set aside for the project.

The teachers urged the administrators who led the project to find ways to allow them to continue learning together and to extend these kinds of experiences to other teachers. They told us there was little point in wasting time and energy on traditional forms of inservice in which teachers participate in workshops but usually lack the insights or time to apply anything new in the classroom. They said it was important to them to have a choice about whether to participate in a project or not and to work with a relatively small group at the start. They talked about how few times in the past they had felt like professionals. Some spoke passionately about the pressures they feel to do a good job and to have children achieve, and they also spoke about the lack of time to accomplish what needs to be done. They talked about the lives some of their children lead and about how powerless they feel to effect change. They said being part of the project made them feel less alone and more supported.

I was not surprised at the success of this project. It embodied the principles of whole language teaching and the messages of research on teacher change. The teachers' learning experiences were reflective of all of the whole language beliefs I listed in the Introduction.

1. *Learners actively construct meaning by relating information to their prior knowledge.* The project leaders assumed that the teachers already had insights and understandings about how to support children's literacy learning. Throughout the project, there were many opportunities for participants to share this prior knowledge and to build upon it by connecting new information to what they already knew.

2. *Learning occurs through the active involvement of learners in generating and testing hypotheses, seeing patterns and relationships, and making connections.* The project was structured around each teacher's work with one student. The leaders encouraged the teachers to work through a problem-solving process as they gathered assessment information, tried out different ways of supporting their learners' needs, and reflected upon the results. Through this process, they generated new insights about literacy learning.

3. *The learner's purposes and intentions determine how, when, and what learning occurs.* The teachers had opportunities to shape this learning experience in ways that made sense to them. The project was designed to respond to professional development needs that the teachers themselves had identified. The leaders resisted the temptation to take over.

4. *Learning occurs through the learner's direct involvement in and reflections upon a wide range of experiences.* The teachers learned more about helping readers and writers by trying out different forms of support and reflecting upon the outcomes. They talked, read, and wrote about what they were learning. They brought their school experiences to the

wider discussions at the district level. The leaders continually asked questions that encouraged group sharing and reflection.

5. *Learning is social.* The teachers participated in many different social contexts. The leaders worked very hard to share power and authority and to invite participants to voice their diverse perspectives and opinions. It was clear from the teachers' comments that the opportunity to collaborate at the school level and with the larger group was to them the single most important influence on their learning.

At the conclusion of the first year of the project, we had collected ample evidence to demonstrate the efficacy of this approach to staff development. As I write, we are looking forward to a second year in which we will need to find ways to sustain and extend the project, despite district-wide fiscal restraints. I still have control over some funds for substitutes, so I can offer a small amount of support. We are exploring partnerships with teacher education institutions to involve faculty and student teachers in the project. The schools that are moving into their second year in the project are devising ways they might create release time and opportunities for teaming through innovative scheduling. I am reluctant to become too ambitious or to expand too quickly. All who become involved will need as much time and space as the four schools did in the first year. We have to resist the temptation to put our experienced teams on the road to provide step-by-step procedures for others to follow. The most they can do is talk about the process and to help other schools replicate the conditions within which change and growth are most likely to occur. If schools and school districts really are serious about improving student learning, we must listen carefully to the voices of these teachers, who can now speak so eloquently and powerfully about their own needs as learners.

Meanwhile, the conversations about oral language and literacy learning continue. Lynne Healy recently shared with me her concern that, despite our attempts to help teachers understand the role of phonology as only one of four interrelated language systems, there is the misconception that attention to sounds is all children need to progress as readers and writers. Lynne and Susan Jozsa, another of our speech language pathologists, have been discussing how some children's lack of awareness of syntactic relationships clearly impedes their understanding of texts, as they miss the essential connections within and among phrases, clauses, sentences, and paragraphs. Bringing attention to the grapho-phonic system led some to believe we were advocating phonics instruction. Will a focus on syntax breathe new life into the teaching of formal grammar? Or if we raise the issue of semantics, will it signal a return to drill on lists of new vocabulary? To open the conversations about language/literacy development in ways that will lead to productive growth, rather than a return to former practices, we need to create contexts like that of the literacy project—contexts within which all of us can continue to generate new questions.

Within the district and province, our small project of possibility stands amidst an array of initiatives competing for time and resources. It represents an alternative vision of professional development. I see evidence of similar efforts within some schools in which administrators and teachers have made a commitment to long-term inquiry into a topic that is of concern and interest to them and their communities. A number of schools have decided to develop their science curriculum, and several have chosen to bring a focus on the arts across the curriculum in collaboration with the arts community. I believe all these undertakings provide opportunities for us to revisit language/literacy learning, such as to explore how children learn through and with language in the context of science or to inquire into how they construct and communicate meaning through the visual arts, drama, music, and movement.

At the same time, however, the province is engaged in major curriculum reform in conjunction with the other Atlantic provinces. It has promised that Pan-Canadian curriculum will soon be in the offing. Program changes are starting to trickle their way down into schools in the form of new guidelines. There are an increasing number of provincial and national assessments in place or under development. Our district has written a strategic plan and has directed all schools to develop site plans over the next few years. The province has established pilot schools for site-based management and is encouraging the formation of school councils. There are ambitious agendas for leadership training to prepare administrators for new responsibilities. The list goes on.

The literacy project and these highly structured, top-down reforms represent fundamentally different views of educational change and teacher learning. For me, as a leader caught up in these conflicting agendas, the most difficult and complex political question of all is whether and how I can critique these high-profile change initiatives without alienating myself totally from the institution within which I work. I believe I must engage in that critique; to do otherwise would be to repudiate the philosophies that have guided my work for many years. Moreover, I believe I must move beyond critique to take action where it is possible to do so. In taking up this rather large and risky project of possibility, which is the subject of the next chapter, I am guided by the following quote from Carolyn Heilbrun (1988):

> Many of us who are privileged—not only academics in tenured positions, of course, but more broadly those with some assured place and pattern in their lives, with some financial security—are in danger of choosing to stay right where we are, to undertake each day's routine, and to listen to our arteries hardening. I do not believe that death should find us seated comfortably in our tenured positions. (131)

The most liberating thought of all, however, is one that I have recorded where I can see it every day: "we should make use of our security, our seniority, to take risks, to make noise, to be courageous, to become unpopular" (Heilbrun 1988, 131).

∿∿∿ Chapter Six

Negotiating the Slippery Slopes of Organizational Change

The Contradictory Messages of Reform

From what I read in the media and professional literature and what I hear from colleagues in other parts of Canada and in the United States, Nova Scotia is no different from many other jurisdictions; curriculum reform seems to be under way everywhere, and it is happening at a frenetic pace. In this province, there will be a complete revision of programs in language arts, mathematics, science, and French over the next four to five years. Nova Scotia has undertaken this task, along with the development of outcomes and program assessments, in cooperation with the three other Atlantic provinces (New Brunswick, Prince Edward Island, and Newfoundland). Next will come the promised Pan-Canadian curriculum projects. One government employee told me privately that their instructions are to avoid the term "national curriculum" because that idea has come under such fierce attack, especially in Canada, where education has always been a provincial responsibility. Canadians tend to be very suspicious of national anything.

The politicians make quite a point of telling us that this cooperation will result in major cost savings and in better programs that will prepare our students to compete in the world. Beyond that, they seem, unlike public officials elsewhere, to be leaving the content and structure of the curriculum guides and the assessments to the educators. That certainly is a positive feature of the Canadian context. As well, I have a great deal of confidence in the Nova Scotian educators involved in the various projects that are under way. What troubles me, however, is seeing so many material and human resources devoted to work that is clearly being driven by a political rather than an educational agenda. There are few, if any, teachers crying for a total reform of the curriculum. Parents usually have more interest in what is happening in their own children's schools than in what the government says the program should be. I'm not sure if even the media and business critics of education see this development work as a solution to the problems they have identified, although the government is doing its best to convince everyone that the effort is an important part of the cure for the perceived ills of the educational system.

The Nova Scotia curriculum has always been informed by current research, and we have been blessed with many enlightened and visionary leaders at the provincial level over the years. Our curriculum documents carry strong messages about active and experiential learning, inquiry and problem solving, critical thinking, the role of technology, language for learning, and the valuing of diversity. Teachers can draw upon many other sources of information about teaching and learning through the frameworks developed by professional organizations and through journals and books. The difficulties in effecting change have never stemmed from a lack of resources to assist teachers with their work; the problem has always been the structural and organizational one I discussed in the previous chapter. As the history of whole language in Nova Scotia reveals, innovations founder not because they are inadequately articulated in provincial documents, but because there are so many institutional impediments to teacher change.

My critique is not aimed at the individuals who are providing leadership for these development initiatives. I am grateful that such thoughtful and articulate educators have an important role in shaping the agenda that the politicians have imposed. I am even optimistic that students and teachers will benefit from some of their work. I have seen the positive results of a provincial performance assessment in language arts that I helped develop several years ago and that is now administered province-wide every three years. I worked on a committee that devised a ten-session performance assessment in which sixth grade students create a file folder of their draft writing, responses to literature, and, finally, a polished piece. The Nova Scotia Department of Education hires teachers and administrators to holistically score a provincial sample of these writing files and then publishes district and provincial scores, as well as an analysis and interpretation of the rich qualitative data the assessment yields. These scoring sessions have proven to be highly productive learning experiences for those involved, as they engage in professional conversations about literacy learning for ten full days during the summer. As well, the staffs of some schools have analyzed the writing in the files of their own students, using the scoring criteria and anchor papers generated during the provincial scoring. Teachers who have participated in these sessions, whether at the provincial, district, or school level, have indicated that the discussions helped them to articulate much more clearly what they value in students' writing and responses to literature. One veteran teacher told his principal, "I should have done this twenty years ago."

Individual projects such as this language arts assessment clearly have their benefits. Nevertheless, I feel compelled to protest the duplicity of the government that has initiated them. On one hand, it has cut ten percent of the funding to school boards over five years and has broken provincial contracts with the teachers' union; on the other hand, it is engaging in a costly and resource-hungry revision of the curriculum that includes the development of large-scale assessments to monitor the program. It has told schools and communities that they will now have more autonomy over their own destinies through site-based management, yet it is shifting more and more control over curriculum and assessment to the regional and, increasingly, the national level. This has already begun with the recent introduction of nationwide assessments in language arts, mathematics, and science through the School Achievement Indicators Project that was initiated through the Canadian Council of Ministers of Education.

This same pattern has been repeated in many other parts of the world. Smyth (1992), writing from an Australian context, calls this "the rhetoric of devolution in a context of centralism" (270). He describes how the government that came into power in New South Wales in 1984 demonstrated these contradictions: "the rhetoric is that of autonomy and devolution, but the reality is a corporate management model that demands compliance and control" (272). While the escalation of central control over curriculum is extremely worrying, especially since one wonders what accountability measures will accompany it, what is even more troublesome is the claim that this top-down approach will actually benefit students. The government can publish whatever curriculum documents and assessments it wishes, but the evidence shows that schools are resistant to change imposed from on high. The real disservice to students, teachers, and communities is that all this money and time are being devoted to program development efforts that we know, given the history of reform, will not substantially change what happens in classrooms and schools. When we have a growing body of evidence to show us what does seem to promote educational change, it seems cruelly ironic to me that decision-makers continue to waste our precious resources on costly projects that give the appearance of reform.

What worries me even more, however, is that we will go the way of other areas and find the allocation of funding and resources tied to scores on provincial and national testing and ratings on other performance indicators. For a province like Nova Scotia, where there are already great disparities among communities and where these gaps are getting larger because of the collapse of the fisheries and other resource-based industries, that is potentially disastrous. Since we know students' performance on standardized tests and many other success indicators is closely related to the socio-economic status of a community, this linking of resource allocation to performance will only exacerbate inequities and contribute to further disempowerment of our least privileged students and their families. What does this have to do with whole language? I believe part of the reason whole language philosophy is under attack is because those who espouse it resist attempts to impose top-down controls on what happens in their classrooms and schools by vigorously opposing standardized testing, packaged materials, and other forms of coercion. They value and foster the diverse capacities and capabilities of all children, not just of those who have the most potential to contribute to the economy. Their purposes are not primarily to help young people learn to compete in the world; they are more concerned about helping them to understand democratic ideals, to live and work with their differences, and to become productive citizens.

What of the other side of the equation—the devolution of authority to schools and their communities? In many places this is described as control over the "how." Through shifts to various forms of site-based management, governments claim they are empowering schools and their communities to determine how best to use the resources available to help them reach the centrally established goals. For example, in Nova Scotia the central curriculum reform effort is combined with an ambitious program to create site-based managed schools, to involve communities in their schools through school councils, and to eliminate middle-management positions in district offices through the amalgamation of twenty-one districts to seven. This is a classic example of the contradictions named by Smyth, who characterizes the world-wide movement toward site-based management as a means through which governments are divesting themselves of responsibility for solving economic and social problems that resist solutions:

> There have been significant restructurings of education systems worldwide in ways that enable the state to acquire even greater

control over essential functions (especially the power to determine policy and control resources), while simultaneously withdrawing from intervention in areas where it demonstrably cannot
be successful (such as equality of education opportunity and
equality of educational provision). (1992, 279)

Shifts in governance have not, historically, been a productive means through which to improve student learning, which
is the espoused goal of all the reform agendas. In a review of
the history of educational reform in the United States, Tyack
(1993) documents a series of pendulum swings between cen-
tralization and decentralization, none of which resulted in
profound changes in classroom practices. This seems especially true of the current situation in Nova Scotia in which
schools and communities do not have much say over what is
really important: the program students will experience and
the means through which to assess it. Fullan (1993) warns
against looking at change as simply restructuring:

> The hardest core to crack is the learning core—changes in
> instructional practices and in the culture of teaching toward
> greater collaborative relationships among students, teachers and
> other potential partners. Stated differently, to restructure is not
> to reculture—a lesson increasingly echoed in other attempts at
> reform. Changing formal structures is not the same as changing
> norms, habits, skills and beliefs. (49)

As well, there seems to be insufficient recognition of the
complexity of the relationships that need to exist between
schools and the district if the kinds of changes we need are to
occur—changes that result in reculturing, not simply restructuring. After reviewing many school improvement efforts,
Fullan concluded that all successful reform efforts involve
close working relationships between school personnel and
those in support roles outside the school.

My own experiences and my reading of the literature on
educational reform suggest that it is not so much the effort to
shift more responsibility for change to the school level that is
the problem; in fact, there is growing evidence to suggest that

devolution of power is the only means through which teaching and learning *will* improve. My concerns center on the contradictions created by the current political context within which much of this devolution is more apparent than real. I have followed with interest the extensive publicity on the efforts to reform education in the Chicago school system, where a great deal of control has been shifted to schools and communities. Principals have greater authority over school budgets and over the building itself. They are accountable to school councils composed of community members and teachers. The focus of the reform is school improvement through greater local autonomy. A recent in-depth analysis of what has happened in the district's five hundred elementary schools during the first four years of the reform shows varied results (Bryk et al. 1994). Even where changes in attitudes, relationships, and organizational patterns have occurred, there still seem to be no noteworthy improvements in student learning. Recognizing that the reforms are still evolving and cautioning against rushing to judgment too quickly, the researchers point to the need for "a whole new infrastructure to support the work of schools. Unless schools truly become learning environments for adults as well as students, the full potential of the Chicago School Reform Act is not likely to be reached" (77).

I recently met an exceptionally articulate and very angry young teacher from Chicago at a conference session on political issues in education. Her view on school reform is through the windows of an inner-city high school that serves a very needy population of African-American youth. She told me of her frustrations in trying to establish a school-within-a-school that she and three colleagues had designed to provide a more supportive and meaningful environment for one hundred students across three grades. She described how the move to site-based management dismantled the district administrative hierarchy, but how an equally cumbersome and authoritarian bureaucracy was rising in its place to control the funding for individual schools and for innovative projects such as hers. She said, "Nobody really wants to give teachers power. They still want to control what we do. And they sure don't seem to care about our kids. The budget cuts hit us the hardest. With a voucher system, we're dead."

Even if I were convinced that restructuring efforts were truly aimed at sharing control and decision-making, I would still have many questions about the beliefs that underlie the methods for achieving that end. Many of these methods seem to be based upon simplistic, reductionist models of learning. Strategic planning models, many staff and community training programs, and approaches to leadership development strike me as quite similar to skills-based models of learning: they are linear, incremental, and sequential. They seem, at times, to be an end in themselves rather than a means to an end; often those who lead them fail to take into account the meanings and purposes participants might bring to the learning situation. Even when the planning or training activities themselves are participatory, the overall enterprise is dominated by those who set the agenda and impose the processes and procedures through which that agenda will unfold.

Many of these approaches seem very like grammar lessons. There is substantial evidence that teaching students the structures and forms of language outside the context of writing, before writers have determined they have something to say and someone to whom they wish to say it, is not an effective way to improve writing. It seems equally wrongheaded to prepare teachers and administrators to work with their communities by training them in conflict resolution, consensus building, and priority setting before those educators and their communities have determined they have purposes for working together and conflicts they need to resolve. In teaching writing within a whole language philosophy, we have learned to begin with the writer's desire to express meaning—in the case of young children, when they first begin to use scribbles in their journals or in notes and letters to peers or adults. The children's knowledge of grammar and other language conventions develops through use, but also through the lessons provided by parents and teachers as they assist the children in solving problems they encounter and respond to questions children ask.

It seems to me we would be much further ahead in advancing collaborative cultures in schools if we focused more on the purposes of that collaboration—the improvement of teaching and learning—before we leaped to training staff and community members in its forms. It is clear that information about language form is much more likely to stick with writers if they see a real need for it—if they care enough about what they are writing to grapple with form in order to express their ideas with more power, clarity, and grace. Similarly, I believe that schools and communities that truly want to work together on behalf of their students will find ways to do so using what they already know, and that they will acquire additional skills such as conflict resolution, consensus building, and others as they need them. To focus on the skills first is as counter-productive as beginning writing instruction with grammar and spelling lessons.

In short, I maintain that the necessary reculturing of organizations has more to do with what those involved believe than with what specific skills they bring to the process. The skills are relatively easy to learn; it is the purposes for behaving differently and the will to make the attitudinal and behavioral changes that are central. If administrators use conflict resolution and consensus building techniques to ram a pre-ordained agenda down the throats of teachers and parents, how does that change anything? Moreover, if only middle- and upper-class parents become part of the conversations within the school, it seems to me that collaboration can be used to promote inequities rather than improved learning for all. I have observed a number of schools in my own district move through site-planning, site-based management, the formation of parent advisory councils, and other efforts to involve staff and community in thinking through future directions for the school. The most exciting developments seem to be occurring where leaders come with a predisposition toward sharing control and truly believe in the power of collaboration. In schools where administrators and staff have only embraced the forms associated with collaboration by applying a set of procedures or a particular planning model, the schools look very much as they did before—with attitudes, roles, relationships, and structures pretty much unchanged. Where change does occur in these situations, it appears to be superficial, first-order tinkering with what is rather than second-order transformation to what could be. The change appears very much like the examples of "whole language dress-up" that I referred to earlier.

Just as curriculum leaders in Nova Scotia in the 1980s who attempted to implement whole language underestimated the time, energy, and resources required to assist teachers in learning a different way to work in the classroom, would-be reformers—including the many governmental bodies now promoting change—seem to continue to look for quick-fixes and easily implemented packages that will achieve restructuring, even with the mounting research evidence that suggests this approach is doomed to failure. I believe that alternatives, like the literacy project described in Chapter Five, have much more potential to move us forward. Not only did the project help to transform norms, habits, skills, and beliefs among the school teams involved, but it also showed the important roles of those outside the school in fostering that change. Ongoing interactions among the schools and the supervisory staff on the steering committee helped to sustain the school teams by supporting and validating their work. Moreover, the meetings of the steering committee and of the entire project team created a context within which participants generated new questions, diverse perspectives, and alternative points of view that then informed the work within the schools.

I think those of us who understand whole language theory and attempt to apply it in our work, whether we are teachers, principals, or superintendents, have a great deal to contribute to the current restructuring movement. Most of us, having struggled to create and sustain collaborative environments in classrooms, understand the complexities and constraints of that work. Our voices need to be heard in the current conversations about school renewal; we need to use our insights and expertise to help shape that unfolding agenda. The present context, while fraught with contradictions and replete with change efforts that resemble grammar lessons, also provides us with openings and opportunities. As a whole language teacher, I can make sense of Hargreaves' (1994) discussions about postmodern organizations because his description of these organizations mirrors how I might describe a successful whole language classroom:

> The kinds of organizations most likely to prosper in the postindustrial, postmodern world, it is widely argued, are ones characterized by flexibility, adaptability, creativity, opportunism, collaboration, continuous improvement, a positive orientation towards problem-solving and commitment to maximizing their capacity to learn about their environment and themselves. (63)

One of the major challenges in the classroom is balancing the collective needs, interests, and perspectives of a community of learners with the unique and specific needs, interests, and perspectives of its individual members. The same skills are needed to meet the challenges of creating space and opportunities for schools and communities to shape their own futures within a larger organization that operates from a shared set of fundamental democratic beliefs in equity, social justice, and freedom. I have learned a great deal from struggling to create an environment in which the diverse perspectives of children could be heard, but also could be questioned and challenged. I bring that prior knowledge to the difficult task of forging more open and collaborative relationships among staff members in a school and between school staffs and their communities. Whole language teaching gives us experience in finding ways to make learning meaningful and purposeful for learners from diverse cultural and linguistic communities. It gives us first-hand knowledge of living with contradictions, uncertainties, and risks. It makes us more comfortable than others in living and working in a postmodern world, which my colleague Blye Frank has suggested is like walking on slippery slopes.

Moving beyond classrooms to promote the restructuring and reculturing of schools and school systems is a vital and necessary part of the political agenda of whole language. It is only through this transformation that we will create conditions of learning for all teachers that will reflect whole language principles and thus foster their ongoing growth. It is only through opening the context for teacher inquiry, dialogue, and reflection that we will increase the numbers of teachers who build their classroom practices on a theoretical framework that is continually informed by what they are learning from their students, by their collaboration with colleagues, and by their active consideration of the professional literature. The only way to counteract the negative effects of the back-to-basics movement is to make its assumptions problematic for parents and teachers. It is only within recultured organizations that we will be able to engage parents in the kind of dialogue and interaction that will be needed for them to become partners in a learning process so unlike the one most of them experienced. It is only in this kind of organization that whole language can ever reach its potential as a force for social change.

Leading the Way/New Ways of Leading

Part of the reason I decided to apply for a supervisory position, and more recently, for a job as an assistant superintendent, was to work in that larger arena beyond the classroom. I became convinced that I needed to move up in the hierarchy in order to contribute to its restructuring and reculturing. I was intrigued by the possibilities for becoming a "whole language supervisor" (different from a supervisor of whole language) and, lately, for positioning myself as a "whole language senior manager." Of course, in reality it is impossible for me to be anything else; I continue to be guided by the principles of teaching, learning, and living that underlie whole language. Leading in organizations undergoing reculturing and restructuring means questioning many of the assumptions that traditionally have driven school and school district administrators. It means trying to keep your feet on the slippery slopes of an ever-changing environment. It means understanding that restructuring and reculturing are never-ending and recursive processes, not ones through which we will arrive at some new right answer about how best to organize. Tewel (1995) suggests that effective leadership in these new organizations means operating without the traditional structures that vest powers with individuals by virtue of their positions in the hierarchy: "Success now depends on figuring out whose collaboration is needed to act on good ideas. In short, the new work implies very different ways of obtaining and using power and influence" (66).

In my own district, those in leadership roles are at many different places in our shift to more collaborative ways of working. Those of us who have provided program leadership over the years certainly have an advantage—most of us have had to rely on the power of influence rather than of line authority. Despite the collective efforts of district leaders to become less hierarchical, the old structures, practices, and relationships are resistant to change. Because I am a member of senior management, sometimes I am implicated in decisions that contradict what I believe. The decisions I find most problematic are those that reflect an authoritarian or coercive stance. When I argue against the imposition of top-down authority, it is sometimes initially seen as an unwillingness to be "tough." Yet I am determined to point out the contradictory messages we send when, as leaders in a system that espouses a flattening of the organization, we continue to speak and behave in authoritarian ways. Often I focus on the language we use. For example, after listening to participants in a meeting talk about "information going down through the system," about staff "in positions below us," or about "communicating with subordinates," I might make a comment like, "For an organization that is flattening, we sure sound like a hierarchy. Maybe we should say information flows out into the system, that individuals work with us, and that we communicate with others in our departments." Because the organization is trying to reculture, I have never had anyone react negatively or defensively to this kind of reminder. On the contrary, they usually acknowledge that they have slipped back into old habits and often lighten the situation with humor, "So, you think stomping on people is a bit top-down, do you?"

Increasingly, I am also bringing a gender analysis to my work. Like most school districts across North America, ours is primarily administered by men. By 1993 only a little more than 7 percent of superintendents, 24 percent of assistant superintendents, and 34 percent of principals in the United States were female (Montenegro 1993). In Canada the statistics are comparable. Within my own district, I am the only female assistant superintendent among a group of five who report to our male superintendent. I am grateful that the senior management team also includes the communications manager, who is female. The three school supervisors at the next administrative level are also male. While I have good working relationships with these male colleagues, I do seem to see the world differently from most of them. Feminist researchers Gosetti and Rusch (1995) describe precisely the way I feel:

> As educational leaders, many women experience a landscape to which they are truly strangers; a landscape dominated by a culture of privileged, white, male leadership which sets the standards and norms of the education profession. Although they have achieved insider status, these women do not feel comfortable embracing many of the activities, values and beliefs of the dominant leadership culture. In essence, these women have a foot in two worlds: the center and the margin. (15)

That sense of marginalization is stronger at some times than others. I have learned to expect the differences. As Gosetti and Rusch maintain, female leaders in working situations like mine "not only experience a different reality than the dominant group, but also provide a different interpretation of reality" (15).

The ways of leading that seem to come easily and make the most sense to me and most of my female colleagues are those that respected researchers say are needed in collaboratively run organizations. For example, Fullan and Hargreaves (1991) conclude from their reading of the research that

> women's socialization prepares them better to develop and lead such organizations. Women tend more than men to negotiate conflict in ways that protect ongoing relationships (as opposed to seeing conflict in win-lose terms), and they tend to value relationships in and of themselves as part of their commitment to care (rather than seeing relationships as instruments to other purposes). (61)

Sergiovanni (1992) paints what he calls a new mindscape for leadership. He characterizes the role as one of a steward or servant rather than as one of a manager, and he envisions empowerment as "power to" rather than "power over" others. He, too, raises the gender issue: "Power *to*, for example, is an idea close to the feminist tradition, as are such ideas as servant leadership and community. By contrast, the more traditional conceptions of leadership seem decidedly more male-oriented" (135). Schein (1992), the pioneer researcher and theorist on organizational culture, believes the organizations of today and the future need leaders who themselves are learners and who can create learning organizations. He suggests women may have particular strengths to bring to this kind of leadership:

> It is also worth noting that in many cultures, notably Western ones, the assumption that one knows and is in control is particularly associated with masculine roles. It is quite possible that

women as leaders will find it easier to accept a whole range of methods for arriving at solutions and will therefore be more able in a learning role. (367)

Feminist researchers, however, suggest that women should respond to these sorts of endorsements with some caution. The professional literature is still dominated by males who interpret how females lead and who frequently seem to make the assumption that there is a generic female leader. Research by women (Dunlap and Schmuck 1995), on the other hand, reveals a complex and diverse range of perspectives and styles among women in leadership roles. While many of these women reject the traditional command and control approaches to leadership, once highly valued in hierarchical institutions, they are by no means all the same. As well, there is increasing evidence that many men, too, find themselves alienated from the traditional ways of leading. Helgeson (1995) describes the flood of mail that she received from men following the publication of her earlier book, *The Female Advantage* (1990), in which she contrasted the leadership practices of several female business executives with those associated with traditional male leadership styles. Her male respondents pointed out how they "had grown disillusioned with traditional chain of command leadership through watching their own companies flounder because of bad decisions made by insulated executives handing directives down from the top" (1995, 11).

While it is clear that white males, because of their dominant positions in most organizations, have had a powerful influence over structures and leadership styles, it is an oversimplification to suggest that all females or only females have special insights into how to lead differently. I hope that we are making progress in valuing the diverse perspectives brought to leadership by women, by individuals from nondominant racial and cultural groups, and by men who reject the dominant white male leadership culture. I know, however, just how pervasive are the values and assumptions of that culture, even among women and men who resist them. As an optimist, I like to think that a recognition of women's strengths, however oversimplified that recognition might be, will make school systems more hospitable to female leaders. The question seems to be: Does the increasing value placed on female ways of leading signal an age of opportunity for women or "an act of appropriation by the dominant leadership culture?" (Gosetti and Rusch 1995, 22). While I count myself fortunate to work with a number of male colleagues who respect and value what I bring as a female leader, if I am honest I must admit that I know many others who are more likely to co-opt the language of collaboration and empowerment to enhance their own potential for advancement in the system. I doubt that many of them even notice collaboration and empowerment when it is enacted by women.

I am encouraged, however, that at least gender is more openly on the agenda than it was in the past. One of the reasons I am so committed to bringing a critical edge to teaching is that I found myself so ill-prepared by my own schooling to understand how I am positioned by my gender. As I mentioned earlier, I came rather late in life to the realization that norms, attitudes, beliefs, and practices I took as givens were socially constructed—that my experiences and interpretations as a female had as much legitimacy and truth as those of men. I feel it is incumbent upon me as a woman in a leadership role to make gender a topic of inquiry in the organization. I want female teachers and students to see possibilities for themselves as a result of the ways I lead. In collaboration with female and male colleagues I want to help create new norms and values of leadership. This is all part of the larger agenda of social justice and equity that I view as inherent to whole language philosophy. To some it may seem like quite a stretch to embed gender and leadership within a theoretical framework that is associated with the teaching of reading and writing, but it is a comfortable fit within the expanded conception of whole language for which I am arguing.

A Close-up Look at Reform

Our district has taken a proactive stance in the provincial efforts to restructure, eliminating levels of middle management in order to streamline the organization and to shift more resources to the local level. Since the late 1960s, the district of thirty-three thousand students and seventy-five schools, spread over a large and diverse geography, had been divided into regional subsystems for ease of administration. Each subsystem had been staffed with a senior manager and one or more program/service supervisors, depending upon the size of the region, which had included about twenty schools that usually identified more with the smaller unit than with the system as a whole. Over the years there were always tensions among the levels; it was common for schools to be struggling to respond to several competing agendas: their own goals and needs, demands from the subsystem level, and expectations from the system. It was extremely difficult to coordinate activities because the subsystems had a great deal of autonomy. In many respects the district was more like a loosely coupled federation of four districts, and there was a great deal of duplication. As fiscal restraints increased and the province-wide move toward site-based management gathered strength, it became clear that the district was devoting scarce resources to sustain levels of administrative support that were no longer useful or appropriate. Consequently, a major feature of the current restructuring has been the elimination of those regional units.

The change in structure provided a context within which we could rethink how best to provide program and student service supports to schools. I now work with a team of district-level supervisors who increasingly are moving away from rigid role descriptions to more flexible assignments. I have asked the group to reflect upon Barth's (1986) article regarding school reform, which has always been a favorite of mine. In it, Barth critiques the "list logic" of many reform initiatives that lay out agendas for school improvement that have very little to do with how schools might reshape themselves. The success of list logic reforms depends upon teachers and administrators being what Barth calls "bright sheep" who can deal with the complexities of change but who also follow directions from others. The problem is that neither sheep nor people come that way. Barth draws upon his rural background to conclude: "As I learned on the farm, you can have dumb, plodding, pedestrian, undistinguished, compliant sheep—or you can have bright, discriminating, questioning, willful goats. You may have both in one school, but you cannot have both within a single individual" (295). Barth believes we must forget the lists and focus instead on creating communities of learners within schools through fostering goat-like behavior. I have challenged the supervisors to see themselves as goats rather than as sheep and to behave accordingly in their relationships with me, with each other, and with school staffs. They seem energized and excited by the possibilities this challenge holds; I am enjoying being a bit of a goat myself.

We see our major task as helping schools to become continually self-renewing through the development of beliefs, attitudes, roles, responsibilities, structures, and processes that support the learning of both students and adults. We know from the research on educational change that school staffs and those of us who work outside the school need to pay attention to the broader organizational context if the potentials for real change at the school level are to be realized. With that in mind, we have initiated discussions regarding ways groups of schools can share resources and expertise and can assist each other with problem solving. Over time, we hope to allocate resources to these school groupings, such as funds to be used for release time to free teachers for short-term leadership roles and for participation in curriculum projects. There are also plans to give more control over budgets to schools and groups of schools so that they can determine how best to use our increasingly scarce financial resources.

At the district level, supervisory staff are increasingly assuming leadership for specific tasks, both as individuals and teams and in collaboration with school-based administrators and teachers. We are making a concerted effort to shape these task assignments in response to needs identified at the school level. I am personally enjoying the challenge of finding ways to advance the restructuring: sharing information more widely and openly; reducing the number of formal, regularly scheduled meetings; increasing the opportunities for staff to meet informally as needed, often without me; creating more fluid and multi-directional lines of communication; inviting staff to initiate projects, take on new responsibilities, and form different kinds of teams; shifting resources to the local level and relinquishing control of their allocation; promoting and celebrating productive dissension and the sharing of diverse perspectives; asking provocative questions and inviting honest responses; and so on.

I believe literacy educators have some particular advantages in our changing environment. I find my power to effect change is enhanced because I know how to use language effectively. I use talk and writing to get things done. In the summer of 1994, when the government issued a discussion paper on the restructuring of schools, I became so angry at some of the assumptions and directions for the future embodied in it that I spent several days crafting a written critique. I used the research literature on change to argue against their simplistic notions of reform and to point out the shortcomings in their logic. I shared my writing with an organization of women administrators to which I belong, and they decided to submit it as their response to the government document. We blanketed the community with it, sending it to provincial government officials, school board members, district administrators across the province, the media, university administrators, and anyone else we thought would be interested. We were invited to participate in panel discussions on the government document and to conduct workshops on its contents. We used our powers of literacy to get noticed and to be heard.

Because I am a writer, I often create written summaries and reflections following meetings and send them out for information and response. I also use drafts and exploratory musings to invite conversations with others in the organization. While it is still a rarity for me to receive written responses to these invitations, the texts do become part of the dialogue around issues. I hope, as time goes by, others will choose to take up this form of literacy. I think it has great potential for opening new ways of thinking and collaborating. Leaders need to be readers and writers in order to create a context in which ongoing learning and inquiry are valued and celebrated.

My background in whole language philosophy and teaching prepared me well to cope with the challenges I now face. I lack some of the formal education in administration and management that my colleagues have acquired, but I seem better able than many of them to envision the ways we need to live and work in institutions that are becoming less hierarchical and more collaborative. While I look to the professional literature on leadership and organizational change for insights, inspiration, and guidance, I find that much of what they have to say resonates with what I have learned through my nearly twenty-year journey with whole language. For example, not long ago I attended a session for administrators led by Kenneth Leithwood, a researcher who has been looking closely at the characteristics of transformational leaders. Toward the end of the workshop, I asked him if he could offer suggestions to districts about how best to foster the development of transformational leadership within the organization. "Not through five-day courses" was his immediate retort. Elaborating, he suggested that the widespread faith in packaged leadership training programs is misplaced, and that we should instead be finding ways for aspiring leaders to draw upon the support of more experienced leaders to engage in the authentic work the district needs to do.

As I listened to his response, I could not help wondering why it has taken the theories of administrative leadership so long to catch up with those of literacy education. I was reminded of Smith's (1983) notion that children learn to read and write by becoming "members of the club," through apprenticing themselves to more experienced language users. While I was heartened by the researcher's comments, I could not help thinking about the many battles colleagues and I have waged over the years to prevent the investment of time and energy in superficial, one-shot professional development experiences for teachers and administrators. I also speculated about the possible effects his comments were having on those in the room, especially since I knew that some of the workshop participants were sponsors of a five-day training program for leaders that was to take place the following weekend. Since attending that workshop, I have quoted Leithwood whenever it seems appropriate. I find that people seldom totally ignore the insights of such a well-respected expert. At the very least, quoting him gets their attention. It seems too bad that I have to defer to the higher authority of an outside expert to legitimate perspectives that I and many of my colleagues have tried to advance for many years, but that sort of deference seems to be part of the politics of getting heard in the organization.

I enjoy sharing that workshop incident with members of the community of literacy educators that has sustained me over the years. Many of us have moved on to administrative positions in schools and school districts. Often, when I want to discuss issues of organizational leadership, I seek out those longtime colleagues. We now have conversations about the complexities of our present administrative roles that are not unlike the ones we used to have about what to do in the classroom. All of us still seem to see ourselves primarily as teachers as we attempt to orchestrate learning and change in our respective organizations.

There is no shortage of thorny issues to engage my attention as I attempt to teach and lead in ways that are consistent with what I believe. The critical incidents keep coming. The tensions and contradictions intensify. I have come to see that as a healthy sign that we are in a process of transformation. But, when I truly need to ground myself in reality, I seek out the classroom teachers who are part of the community to which I belong. It is they who push my thinking the most and who help me to remember who is really important in this enterprise of schooling—the children. In the next chapter, several of those teacher-colleagues reflect upon what teaching from a critical whole language perspective means to them and to their students.

∿∿ Chapter Seven

Bringing a Critical Edge to Teaching

*I*n the sections that follow, I offer the perspectives of three teachers from among the many I know who continually challenge me to rethink my beliefs and practices. I find my conversations with these colleagues both exhilarating and exhausting. We all seem to be grappling with similar questions about power, authority, language, text, and our own roles within the institution. We all have a history with whole language and struggle with how and where to position ourselves now that we have moved to a more critical stance. I wonder if taking this stance leads us outside whole language to something new or if we can bring the political stance of whole language to the fore. I favor the latter because, as Edelsky (1991) has pointed out, whole language classrooms, not skills-based classrooms, provide the most promising context for promoting social justice and democracy.

Maybe at some point we will agree on entirely different terminology to describe what I am calling critical whole language. I am not so much interested in arriving at agreed-upon terminology, however, as I am in exploring commonalities and differences through ongoing conversations about teaching and learning. Whatever we call what we do, there are many theoretical and practical issues that need our attention. Each of the teachers highlighted below brings a somewhat different perspective to those issues. They do not offer easy answers; they identify many tensions, contradictions, and risks. Nevertheless, they leave me with a strong sense of hope about what is possible when teachers engage in ongoing reflection about their work.

Moving Toward Critical Literacy

Jim Albright and I have had a running discussion about whole language over the past several years. I first met Jim when I was the curriculum supervisor responsible for language arts in our district. Someone gave me Jim's name as a possible workshop leader for inservices related to whole language at the junior high level. During the mid- to late-1980s I had a number of opportunities to talk with him about his efforts to implement a reading/writing workshop in his classroom. He had worked closely with Maureen Gow, the resource teacher in his school, to create a literacy curriculum based upon Atwell's (1987) work. He had purchased an extensive library of young adult books and had engaged his students in a great deal of independent reading and writing. Soon, however, he began asking questions about his own practices. This critical self-reflection became even more focused and intense when he began a graduate program at Mount Saint Vincent University.

In his master's thesis, Jim chronicles the story of his growing doubts about whole language in general and about the reading/writing workshop in particular (Albright 1995). He describes how he came to the realization that some of his students were not enthusiastically embracing literacy as he provided them with opportunities to choose their own books and writing topics. He began to question why the workshop did not function as effectively for all his students as it seemed to in Atwell's book. Even among his white, middle-class students, who presumably should have come with a positive predisposition toward literacy, there was resistance to the invitations he extended. Some students did not demonstrate the high levels of engagement that this kind of teaching was supposed to engender. Some actually preferred skills-based teaching because it was more predictable and safe and because it required less of a personal investment on their part. Jim shares his own classroom stories of student resistance and those of other teachers. He offers the following reflection:

> The stories are charged with bewilderment, frustration and anger. It seems to me my response to these feelings and conflicts has been to try to do what I have been doing better. Yet, addressing the nature of literacy conflicts now seems to me to be a fundamentally more appropriate way of responding to this whole issue. (30)

Jim's efforts to "do what I have been doing better" included a major rethinking of the reading/writing workshop. He recognized that he had applied Atwell's model in a lockstep manner and that this inflexibility had contributed to his difficulties in engaging his students. He realized that the reading/writing workshop was a stance toward literacy learning rather than a program. He also became aware of a need to recast his role within the classroom: "I extended invitations and prepared the environment for the students, but, for many students, I did not sufficiently support, encourage and challenge their engagement" (61). Like many other whole language teachers, Jim worked hard to shift control to his students but, as a result, he stepped too far back from the classroom. He came to understand that the teacher needs to continually negotiate freedom and control in order to sustain engagement and learning. Having made that shift, he reflected further on issues of student voice and freedom and, as a result, moved beyond the improvement of his existing practices toward a critical analysis of whole language.

Jim began to question what he terms "the middle class liberalism" that he believes underlies whole language. He had accepted the premise that "engagement in literacy brings fuller participation in the cultural life of our society" (68), but he had not critically examined how schools participate in perpetuating social inequalities through the privileging of certain forms of literacy. He learned that there was more than one literacy and that different notions of literacy are in conflict in the classroom. He began asking questions like: Whose literacy? For what purposes? Previously, he had bought into the whole language message that the way of engendering students' engagement in literacy is to create a powerful association of reading and writing with pleasure and positive social relationships. For example, in the reading/writing workshop students choose books to read for enjoyment, write on self-selected topics, and then share their responses with a community of readers and writers in the classroom and beyond; the message purports that it is through participation in these kinds of literacy experiences that students are empowered to express their voices and become self-actualized. Some of Jim's students, however, did not always share this view of literacy. Their resistance showed that often their school experiences, even those in whole language classrooms like Jim's, left them alienated and angry rather than engaged. These students did not see the forms of literacy valued in schools as meaningful and purposeful in their own lives. Jim's critical analysis of their resistance led him to the following conclusion about the reading/writing workshop: "the form of literacy which it engenders does not fully appreciate the full impact of power relations in the discourses of schools in society" (90).

Jim argues for a much more critical and political interpretation of empowerment. In his view, whole language empowers students only to participate with the dominant discourses of society; it does not make problematic the power relationships that are the source of the literacy conflicts within classrooms and beyond. He wants to empower students through developing their skills of critical analysis, so that they can both understand and resist the social practices that perpetuate inequalities. He believes we must re-theorize literacy education by bringing language-power issues to the fore as Edelsky (1994) has urged.

Jim's inquiry led him to the work of researchers in the areas of critical literacy (Comber 1993; McLaren 1989; Shor 1992; Lankshear 1994; Fairclough 1992) and of feminist pedagogy (Grumet 1988; Christian-Smith 1993), and to the writing of teachers who have brought social justice issues to the center of the curriculum (Bigelow et al. 1994). He is now in the process of exploring what critical practice might mean in his own classroom—specifically, how he can recast the experiences he offers students in ways that bring the critical questions to the fore. For example, Jim might ask students to read a range of texts on a particular topic or interrogate an individual text in detail and then reflect upon why the topic was written about, how it was written about, what other ways there might be of writing about it, who was the intended audience, and whose interests are served by particular ways of addressing a topic. He also wants his students to understand "the socially constructed nature of their schooling" through other kinds of questions: How did practices of schooling come to be? What alternatives to the everyday school practices could be explored?

Jim is grappling with how best to make a critical stance more explicit. He has organized theme units around social issues, engaged teachers in a graduate education class in critically analyzing a social studies text found in all ninth-grade classrooms in the province, and guided his junior high students through an investigation of language that surfaced questions about the influences of gender, culture, and age on nonverbal communication. In the fall of 1995, Jim returned to an elementary classroom after teaching junior high for a number of years. I spoke with him shortly before school opened and he told me he planned to focus on peace education in his fourth-grade classroom, by using the work of Hetty Adams, an administrator in our district who has provided leadership in this area and has written about how teachers can help children learn to live together in harmony (Adams 1994). Jim anticipated that this inquiry would provide opportunities for students to investigate issues of power, control, and human rights within the context of their own classroom and school.

Jim is very much aware of his own position within the institution. He wonders how his more explicit political stance will affect his relationships with colleagues and the community. Having established a reputation for being innovative and progressive in his teaching, he asks himself if teachers and parents who have tolerated him in the past will now see him "as having gone too far this time" (Albright 1995, 131). He commented to me that he sees himself in danger of "radicalizing himself out the door." I had to agree that he has embarked on a very risky journey, but one that also holds much potential. As I talked with Jim, I thought about the broader institutional context within which he works. His classroom offers a direct challenge to the reformers who envision the school's primary role as training workers to fuel the economy. His students will not unquestioningly accept the dominant discourses of schooling. They will learn skills of critical analysis that they can apply to texts and their own experiences as a means of understanding how both are socially constructed. They may choose to take action against social inequities. All of this will contribute to their growth as critical language users and citizens, but it may also put them and Jim in conflict with the institution and the community. Clearly Jim is not unaware of the dangers but, having made a theoretical shift to critical literacy, he cannot teach in any other way. He has come to realize that literacy by its very nature is conflicted, whether or not we choose to make the sources of those conflicts explicit to ourselves and our students.

Opening Classroom Conversations

Over the years since the introduction of whole language in our district, I have had many requests from teachers wishing to visit effective whole language classrooms. I always seem to put Susan Settle's name at or near the top of my list of suggestions. She has taught several elementary grades and, like Linda Cook, Florence MacLean-Kanary, and Jim Albright, has continued to grow and change. Several years ago, Susan's classroom was featured in a videotape series that the district co-developed with the provincial Department of Education. Based on a print resource for teachers, *The Supportive Classroom: Literacy for All* (1988), the videotape shows how teachers can provide instruction that meets the specific literacy needs of individuals and groups within the classroom. Susan's section demonstrates clearly the way she structures opportunities for students to write and to reflect upon their writing through conferences with her and with each other. On the tape she talks about how she chooses different forms of support based on each student's needs.

In the several years since that taping, Susan has completed a graduate program at Mount Saint Vincent University, and she continues to participate in summer courses and other professional development opportunities. Her studies have led her to explore how she can teach from a more critical perspective. She believes whole language created the spaces in which she could begin to bring critical issues into classroom conversations. She describes it as "being more open to the issues children themselves raise." It is not so much a matter of initiating critical conversations by posing questions for students, but of helping students to explore their own responses and questions through critical analysis. She has used her recent professional reading related to inquiry to help her think through how best to support students' investigation of questions that interest them.

Susan believes that teaching critically is not so much an approach as a way of being and thinking. The most important aspect of this kind of teaching is that the teacher must be critically aware in order to respond to what arises. The issues are all around us: in conflicts that occur on the playground, in the social life of the classroom, and in the texts teachers and students read and write. She sees her role as helping children to look beneath the surface of their experiences and of texts to explore the deeper social issues. From time to time, she chooses books with social themes to read aloud to the students, but she tries not to be too leading in the way she engages children in conversations about those books. She begins with open-ended questions: So, what did you think? How did that make you feel? She tries to stay out of the discussion initially and does not force it in particular directions if students do not raise the issues that seem important to her. Once children offer comments or questions, she and the students explore the issues further. For example, a science-fiction book she read aloud surfaced strong feelings about gender, so Susan extended the children's comments through further discussion. She encouraged the class to return to the story to consider which characters had power, which did not, and how the author positioned them as readers. This led to further conversations about gender issues in the children's own lives.

Susan is very much aware of the tensions created through the exploration of these kinds of questions. She continually asks herself, How far do we go with this? She believes teachers must know their students well and monitor their reactions. She described what happened recently when the class was discussing a seemingly safe topic:

> There had been an incident on the news about a child in our community who had saved another one from drowning after he fell through the ice. I decided to take the opportunity to discuss hypothermia with the students. After only a brief discussion about what it is and how it affects people, one little boy burst into tears and said, "I don't want to talk about this any more." It turned out he had gotten his feet wet on the way to school and he imagined that he was getting the symptoms of hypothermia as he sat at his desk. That incident reminded me that we have to be very careful how we deal with any topic in the classroom, particularly ones that may be sensitive. We never know what is going on in students' heads.

As an experienced whole language teacher, Susan has thought a great deal about how to help students develop voice. Until she began reading critical theory and discussing its implications for her teaching, the concept of voice remained unproblematized for her. She believed she was listening to children and encouraging them to find their own voices in their writing. She had not thought about the ways voice is socially constructed, so that we can never just speak for ourselves. Our writing and talk reflect a plurality of voices that are shaped by our gender, class, culture, and race. Susan recalls,

> When I started teaching, those were not issues that entered my mind. I was enraptured by the creativity of teaching. I did not think about teacher authority or about my own positioning as a gendered being. I heard about gender but did not connect it to my own life. It was only after I read about gender issues and talked to other people that I began to understand my experiences differently. I looked back on what had bothered me in the past and began to bring a gender analysis to those experiences, such as the ways I had been positioned as a female teacher. I saw that my own reticence to express my views, to use my voice, if you will, was a reflection of my social conditioning as a female. It was only after I learned how to name my own experiences of gender that I began to develop voice.

Susan continually reflects upon issues of power and control in the classroom and beyond. Several years ago Andy Manning, a teacher-educator from Mount Saint Vincent University with whom she has studied extensively, posed a question that she feels was pivotal in her growth. He asked, Can anyone in your classroom call a meeting? As she thought about the question, she realized that the subject had never come up in her classroom. While she had thought she was sharing control with students, she had not brought the power relationships within the classroom into the open. She now is much more explicit about inviting students to call meetings and to shape the classroom agenda in other ways. She is more consciously aware of how her position of authority in the classroom puts up barriers to the students' taking control of their learning. She struggles with how to negotiate these issues. She questions some of the versions of critical teaching that seem very teacher-directed. She worries about critical literacy becoming a programmed curriculum with prescribed sets of critical questions to ask.

As she has become more critically aware, Susan has found it more challenging to find common ground with colleagues. Since she began acquiring other discourses, for example becoming conversant with critical theory, she has found it more difficult to talk about teaching with those who have not begun to think about critical awareness or classroom authority in the way she has. She tries to find ways of bridging the differences to avoid alienating herself within the school. I suggested to her that the way she works in the classroom and relates to the children could be a source of alienation from other staff members without her even saying anything about what she believes or does. Susan nodded in agreement and commented rather ruefully, "I really don't see myself as radical."

Susan works very hard to involve parents in their children's schooling. She realizes that critical teaching has the potential to create misunderstandings and conflicts between home and school. She sets aside blocks of time at the beginning of each school year to meet with parents to discuss their wishes for their children. She tries to get to know them and to involve them in decision making about their children's learning. She asks them to share concerns and to let her know if there are aspects of the program that they find problematic and in which they would prefer that their children not participate. These conversations help to lower the stress level for Susan considerably, as she and the parents establish good working relationships from the start. Early and ongoing communication lessens the likelihood that either Susan or her students' parents will experience unpleasant surprises during the year.

Although I have always found Susan to be a reflective teacher, I see a new depth in her understanding of the complexities and contradictions of critical practice. I know she struggles every day with questions of power and authority in her classroom; there is no prescription for this kind of work. Both she and Jim are exploring the subtleties of raising the critical issues without dominating the classroom agenda. Jim is shifting the balance toward more active teacher involvement, but he is clearly cautious about how far to go. Susan seems to be challenging herself and her students to push the boundaries of what is possible in a democratic classroom, but she, too, is mindful of the risks. She wants to shift control to the children, but she knows her own role in making that happen is crucial; becoming less directive does not mean becoming less active. These two classrooms are very different, but they have one extremely important characteristic in common: in each situation, the teacher's own critical awareness is the most significant factor in creating an environment in which critical issues are explored. As Susan commented, "Critical teaching is not a program or an approach; it is a way of thinking."

Leading Critically Literate Lives

I received a very similar response when I asked Vivian Vasquez, a teacher of junior kindergarten (three-, four-, and five-year-olds) in Mississauga, Ontario, how she sees critical literacy. She defined it as "learning to live a critically literate life." She added, "As teachers, we become more critical and live it, and we find ways to help children understand the social issues around them. We don't plan this curriculum; it emerges from the children's lives." Despite living some distance from Nova Scotia, Vivian is an integral part of our community of literacy educators. Several years ago she joined a group of teachers and administrators who were studying in a graduate program with Andy Manning, other faculty from Mount Saint Vincent, and Jerry Harste from Indiana University. It was possible for Vivian to participate in the program because it was scheduled on periodic weekends rather than during the week. Susan Settle was also part of this group, and she and Vivian became close colleagues and friends. They continue to communicate frequently by fax, phone, and e-mail and to attend summer programs and conferences together. Vivian and I met for the first time at an IRA convention a few years ago, and since then we have found ourselves at many of the same conferences, usually in most of the same sessions.

Although I see Vivian infrequently, she has influenced my thinking in important ways. I am fascinated by the insights she offers about critical whole language with three-, four-, and five-year-olds. She told me a brief anecdote that demonstrates how these young children are becoming critically aware by being keen observers of their environment. The incident occurred after a Mountie had visited the classroom with his police dog and left a poster for Vivian to display. She put it up and did not think very much about it until one day when a little girl commented, "Oh, if you want to be a Mountie, you have to be a boy." Vivian had not noticed that the poster showed only men until this astute young child pointed it out. The little girl's observation gave Vivian the opening to talk about gender issues with the small group of children who also took part in that conversation.

Vivian believes that it is through these daily occurrences that children become more critically aware, not through grand activities designed to teach critical skills. She told me,

> I listen to what they talk about in the various play areas, and I observe the songs and books they choose. I pay attention to the underlying issues within the dramas they create and beneath the comments and questions that emerge throughout the day. I look for opportunities to dig deeper with the students by helping them explore the bigger social issues. Over the past few years there has been a great deal of discussion about the question of the teacher "front-loading" in the classroom, that is, bringing particular issues to the fore. Obviously what I choose to focus on with the children reflects what I am thinking about, but the conversations emerge from the children's own lives. Moreover, I show through my interactions with the children that my agenda is only *an* agenda.

Children always have a choice about whether or not they will be part of any conversation. Vivian rarely, if ever, leads the whole class through a discussion; most of her conversations take place with individuals or small groups who happen to be

109

gathered at the time a critical issue becomes the focus. The classroom is structured so that many different kinds of experiences and conversations are taking place at one time. Vivian and another teacher work as a team and have combined their classrooms to create different kinds of spaces in which children can pursue individual and group inquiries. The teachers set up one room for quieter activities, such as reading and writing, and another for music, drama, and active play. This structure accommodates children who learn better when they have quiet areas to work in and those who need more frequent opportunities to move around. All the children have a great deal of choice about activities and groupings. Groups form on their own as children move through the various areas in the two classrooms.

Like most other schools in the greater Toronto area, Vivian's is culturally diverse. She finds that the open, flexible environment that she and her partner create fosters the development of community among children who bring a wide range of different experiences and perspectives to the classroom. The teachers expect that children will be engaged in different kinds of inquiries on their own and with others and that they will not all learn in the same way or at the same pace. This makes the classroom an inviting and supportive place for all children, not only for children from many different cultural groups, but also for those with physical and mental challenges. In the fall of 1995, Vivian's class included a boy who had significant cognitive and linguistic delays. She prepared for his arrival by thinking through how to organize the classroom activities so he would not feel like an outsider. She moved away from having the whole group gather together and, instead, extended invitations to small groups at different times during the day. For example, she had story time more than once so that he could participate in the experience with a small group. She helped the other children to understand how the child used gestures and sounds to communicate, and they quickly began responding to him and including him in groups.

Vivian told me,

> He continually amazes me. Before he came, I was led to believe
> that he would not know what was going on in the classroom. I
> see him doing things every day that tell me his ability was under-
> estimated. Watching him is a powerful reminder to me that we
> can never really access what is going on in children's heads; we
> need to be careful about making judgments about what is possi-
> ble. This young boy is not supposed to be able to read, yet I saw
> him go over to the bulletin board one day and staple his drawing
> under the label with his name on it. Not only that, he had
> figured out how to use the stapler by watching other children.
> Another day, when I was on duty on the playground, I saw him
> kick a soccer ball outside the pylons we had put in place to keep
> the children within a safe play area. I called to him to remind
> him not to go outside the barrier, and he proceeded to move a
> pylon outside the spot where the soccer ball had landed and then
> picked up the ball. From my observations, he certainly seems to
> know a great deal more than he is supposed to know.

Vivian recognizes that she enjoys more freedom from institutional constraints than teachers of older children who often have more rigidly defined curricular expectations that they
must meet. She, too, however, must function within a larger
organization that places demands on her. For example, all
teachers in her school are required to submit yearly plans of
the themes they will cover. During 1995–96, she and her partner met this requirement by choosing the broad theme "Celebrating Diversity." Within that theme, the teachers and
children engage in smaller inquiries, such as "We Grow in
Different Ways" and "I Have Questions About the World."
The children's introduction to writing comes through their
exploration of "Things on Paper Tell Something." This approach to themes is quite different from that of many of the
other teachers, who focus on narrower topics, such as animals
or particular holidays. This does set Vivian apart within the
school. However, she is encouraged that a number of the
teachers in the school are involved in an external graduate
program that is being offered in Toronto by faculty from

Mount Saint Vincent University, in collaboration with Jerry Harste. Vivian is providing local leadership for that program. She finds that colleagues who might have dismissed her comments and questions in the past are now more likely to explore ideas with her. The community of inquiry among the teachers within the school is expanding through these professional conversations.

Vivian invites parents to be active participants in the classroom. To keep them informed about what is happening in school, she regularly sends home a newsletter. When issues like the comments about the Mountie poster come up, she writes about it in the newsletter. She finds that parents in turn often bring issues that concern them to her attention, and that home and school conversations spill over into each other. For example, one little girl was quite surprised to learn that a woman had taken over her father's job for a period of time when he was away. After discussing the topic with her parents, she raised it in the classroom. As a result, a small group of children talked with Vivian about whether that could happen in school. If a boy were away, could only a boy take his place? Could a girl substitute for a boy? A boy for a girl?

Recently, Vivian was grateful that she had created open lines of communication with the parents; another child, contemplating an illustration of God in white robes, asked if God could be a woman since he wore dresses. As a teacher in a Catholic school, Vivian might have had reason to be concerned that parents would have problems with her making that question a subject of further inquiry. Instead, she found that parents responded with interest when she shared the story in the newsletter. As she told me,

> The parents know that the children have a choice about whether to participate in conversations about social issues and that they as parents can always talk to me about concerns they might have. I make it clear to them that my agenda is not the only agenda in the classroom. That seems to make them much more receptive to the way I teach.

The Illusion of Safety

One of the ways I used to characterize whole language teaching was to describe the classroom as a place in which it is safe to take risks. By that I meant that children could try something new and not be afraid to make mistakes. For example, they could express their ideas in writing without being able to spell every word. They could choose writing topics and books and explore these in ways that made sense to them. Unquestionably, I still believe that children should learn in an environment in which they can experiment, make choices, and feel safe from physical or emotional harm. Beyond that, however, I think it is naive to believe that we can create a safe place for learning. By choosing not to make the critical issues central to the curriculum, we can, perhaps, create the illusion of safety. It can appear that learning in the classroom can be confined to seemingly safe topics and that literacy learning itself is unproblematic. After all, the most contentious issue in many quarters seems to be whether phonics is part of the reading program. As teachers, we can close our eyes and ears to the social issues that lie beneath children's questions and comments. When our "safe" curriculum does not seem to be engaging some of our students, we can call them oppositional or declare them "at risk." We can continue to search for right answers—a new approach, a methodology, a program—that create a greater sense of certainty about our work. We can pretend that society and its institutions, including schools, are not structured to perpetuate inequities based on race, class, gender, ability level, and culture.

Jim, Susan, and Vivian have chosen a different path. Through becoming more critically aware, they have abandoned the illusion of safety and certainty. They also want their students to become critically aware so that they not only understand the social practices that influence their lives and learning, but also can work to change them. These teachers grapple with issues of power and authority in their own classrooms and recognize that such issues will never be resolved. As

Jim responded to my concern that some critical literacy practices seemed to be very teacher-dominated, "This is a real
juggling act, where you are always right and always wrong.
What I am suspicious of is how students' questions and input
is socially constructed (just like the teacher's). Both need to be
challenged by critical kinds of tactics and questions. As a critical literacy teacher, I have a stance, no answers."

Jim's quote "you are always right and you are always
wrong" is one both he and I have heard many times from
Judith Newman, who attributes it to Peter Elbow (Newman
1991). It is reflected in Susan's concerns about how directly
she should address critical issues with her students. It is part
of Vivian's discussion of "front loading"—she describes an
active role for herself in helping children dig beneath the
surface of issues, but is cautious about imposing her agenda
on children. I see it in my own work as I try to determine
how best to critique the social practices of the institution.
From time to time, we all long for the certainty and safety of
right answers. I wish at times that I did not see and hear the
critical issues so clearly—that I could live and work with
fewer tensions, contradictions, and risks. But as Vivian said to
me, "Once you become critically aware and live it, you no
longer have a choice. You can never not be in. And once you
start living this way, you recognize it is not safe, because
social justice is not a safe topic. There is no way to provide
safety for students or teachers."

The beliefs and practices espoused by these teachers look
and feel like whole language. It strikes me, however, that it is
a much more "grown-up" version—one that is less naive and
trusting. In this more critical version, it is no longer possible
to talk or write about using "authentic" texts or writing on
"personally meaningful" topics. That language is loaded with
assumptions that need to be examined. Authentic to whom
and for what purposes? What difference does it make when a
text is read in school as opposed to on the bus, in one's living
room, or on the beach? How is a writer's personal meaning
socially constructed? How does the text position the author

and the reader? These are difficult and complex questions, but ones that I believe need to be asked. If we do not, it seems to me that we are in danger of relegating whole language to just another method for teaching reading and writing to dominant groups. It will be a means of perpetuating *what is* rather than a philosophy with the potential to transform.

Like Susan Settle, I have never seen myself as a radical, but in today's political and social context, working for equity and social justice seems to be a revolutionary stance. We educators who choose to take that stance put ourselves at odds with the dominant discourse of the institution. We question the current emphasis on regulation, accountability, and standards. As Vivian expressed it, "It seems as if education is now about policy and procedures, not about people and life."

Most of us became educators because we cared about children and young people, and we wanted them to have the best lives possible. While it may seem risky to fight against the institution, we take even greater risks if we choose not to resist. As I hope I have made clear, I believe whole language educators have a responsibility to take up this political agenda. It does not have to be nearly so risky if we work at it together. In my final chapter, I offer encouraging examples of how this is beginning to occur.

∿ Chapter Eight

Hopeful Signs and Projects of Possibility

There are a great many reasons to be discouraged about working as an educator these days. As I write this in September 1995, the teachers, students, and parents in my district are just beginning to experience the results of severe budget cuts that took place last spring. We have more than eight hundred new students in our schools and more than sixty fewer teachers. Some high school teachers are responsible for two hundred and fifty (or more) students who come to them in classes of over forty. The government reform agenda continues to move forward despite the critical responses of many of those affected by the changes. The amalgamation of school boards is being imposed on districts, some of whom accepted the government's invitation to shape their own futures and arrived at local consensus regarding alternatives to full amalgamation. These alternative structures created efficiencies without destroying the integrity of community-based administrative units, but the government proceeded with full amalgamation anyway. While the government has created the appearance of consultation by inviting response to their proposals and by holding various kinds of focus groups and public meetings, there is a strong sense that there is a preordained agenda that will unfold despite the efforts of many to change it.

I remember feeling this way five years ago when I attended the summer institute with Patrick Shannon. The budget cuts were just beginning in Nova Scotia at that time, and the participants in the course told many stories about the coercive ways in which those in authority were making decisions. Since then, as I have lived through even more draconian fiscal restraints and the imposition of government reforms, it has been helpful to recall the conversations we had with Patrick regarding our situation. He acknowledged the legitimacy of our concerns and our anger, but he also helped us to see the futility in what he termed our "whining." He challenged each of us to find ways in which we could act within the spheres of influence available to us. Judith Newman suggests that the way to sustain energy and purpose is to pick three projects worth doing and to gain satisfaction from accomplishing them. Since then, I have tried to find those areas in which I can take action and to encourage others to do the same. As I pay more attention to the political, I see some evidence that educators, particularly literacy educators, are more prepared to take an overtly political stance. It seems to me that there are promising beginnings taking place upon which we can build.

First, I am encouraged that there appears to be a stronger sense of the political at literacy conferences. Both Patrick Shannon and Carole Edelsky have brought powerful political messages to NCTE and IRA conferences over the past several years. Audiences have come to expect this from Patrick, in particular, but there are others from whom it might be less expected. For example, at the 1994 NCTE fall conference, Donald Graves delivered a much more overtly political speech than I had heard him make before. He spoke eloquently about his concern that our approaches to teaching writing too often destroy voice. He shared his observations that the voice many teachers strive to develop is an exclusionary one that allows no other, and he called for teachers to ask different kinds of questions about voice: Can this voice tolerate others? Can it bring in another point of view and value differences? How much can we tolerate a range of voices? Can we take in a range of perspectives and diverse opinions? How can we ensure that a multiplicity of voices get heard? Graves also talked about the effects of institutional practices on teachers' voices, about the need to show children the meaning of "reading the world," and about forms of assessment that extinguish voice.

There seem to be many more conference sessions that focus on the relationships among gender, race, class, culture, and the teaching of literacy. I have participated in a number of pre-conference sessions and other special workshops designed to provide a forum for the discussion of political issues. The NCTE/SLATE (Support for the Learning and Teaching of English) Steering Committee on Social and Political Concerns sponsors conference workshops and publishes a very reader-friendly and accessible newsletter that highlights current issues. Colleagues and I have attempted to influence conference agendas by submitting proposals for sessions that have a political slant. While these sorts of sessions are not always the most popular with conference attendees, I have found that every presentation has provided me with interesting conversations with people who share my concerns. Each has also helped me to explore different aspects of the issues through engaging in dialogue with others.

The Whole Language Umbrella (WLU), an organization founded in the late 1980s to support networking and research within the whole language community, also has some very outspoken members who are raising political questions. At the organization's 1995 summer conference, a large group gathered for a meeting of the Political Awareness Interest Action Group. This committee's goals include developing ways to support teachers who are working to employ democratic principles in the classroom and encouraging members to take various kinds of political action. I was encouraged to see that this political group seemed to be gathering support within the WLU, because I believe that this organization has not played an active enough political role. Until very recently, it did not seem to be aware of the difficulties being experienced by whole language educators across North America. Conference programs reflected an overwhelming emphasis on pedagogical issues and made it seem that the enactment of whole language within the educational institution was unproblematic as long as teachers had sufficient background in whole language theory. The meeting of the Political Awareness Interest Action Group provided ample evidence that individuals who clearly *are* well-grounded in whole language theory are struggling to sustain themselves in the current context. Some of us talked about the importance of keeping the work of these sorts of action groups going, but also about our difficulty in finding time and energy to do so as we all fight our individual battles in our own communities. I left that meeting with a commitment to myself to try to make some kind of contribution to sustaining the work of the group.

A second area of promise is the publication of articles and books that address political issues in education. My own writing has been one of the most significant means through which I have become more political. Increasingly, I have recognized the power of writing to influence and persuade. I know how useful I have found the series of articles Gerald Bracey (1991, 1992, 1993, 1994) has published in the *Phi Delta Kappan* over the past several years. Each fall he has provided his own "report card" on public education, refuting the allegations that the system is failing. I have been impressed by the way in which he crafts his arguments and uses the research evidence to support them. In the first article of his series, Bracey pointed out that the data he used is available to any interested person. I found myself wondering, why aren't more of us using it?

In their book *Class Warfare* (1994), Maude Barlow and Heather-jane Robertson offer a similar analysis of the Canadian educational scene, where the rhetoric about schools is much the same as in the United States. They show how the results of international tests have been interpreted to make students' performance look much worse than it really is. They critique the efforts of corporations to turn schools into marketplaces for consumer goods and the tactics of representatives of the religious right, who are striving to gain control over the curriculum. Since the book's publication, both authors have been in demand as speakers across Canada. They have provided educators with the language and the data to support their arguments on behalf of public schooling. The book has raised the ire of those who are the brunt of its critique, and it has opened new kinds of conversations about schooling in Canada. While I am not suggesting that everyone can write as powerfully and effectively as Bracey and these two authors, I believe we can all use writing to effect change. As Vivian Vasquez has shown, a relatively small project like a parent newsletter can help to open dialogue, to extend critical awareness beyond the classroom, and to increase parent participation in their children's learning.

A third reason to be hopeful is that there are many examples of strong and supportive working relationships between teacher educators and public schools. Mount Saint Vincent, for example, has been a powerful force for change in literacy education in Nova Scotia. When the institution was recently caught up in a lengthy restructuring of higher education in the province, their presence was sorely missed by the teachers and administrators they had worked with in the school system. While university colleagues have continued to teach and to work with schools when they could, they have been preoccupied with the exhausting negotiations surrounding the consolidation of teacher-education programs. It is only now that the restructuring is over that many of them can turn more of their energy back to working with preservice and inservice teachers—and, I hope, with those of us who are trying to gain more of a voice in the current struggle over the future of public education in Nova Scotia.

The active participation of university-based educators through study groups, formal courses, action research, and collaborative writing has been central to keeping whole language practices grounded in a broadly based theoretical framework—a framework that is continually renewed through inquiry into teaching and learning. While university educators bring many different research interests to their work with teachers, those who have become part of the whole language community seem predisposed to learning with and from teacher-colleagues. In their role as teacher-educators, they grapple with the same issues of power and control as teachers of children and adolescents. They resist the perpetuation of the hierarchical faculty/student relationships that are typical within the university setting, and they work to create different forms of collaboration with teachers and schools. They try to create contexts for adult learners that reflect whole language principles.

I believe that we all need to nurture and enhance these collaborative relationships—not only to sustain ourselves professionally, but also to speak and write with a collective voice. As should be clear from this book, I have been the beneficiary of many such relationships. Most recently, other university colleagues (Church et al. 1994) have also been extremely helpful as I have moved toward a more critical stance.

Clearly, we have all gained personally and professionally from our collaborations. It is interesting to watch how our ways of thinking and talking about the issues can change as our conversations unfold. In addition to learning ourselves, however, we need to move beyond our small groups to share our conversations with a wider audience. It is through more public discourse that we can have an influence on future directions of literacy education and schooling as a whole.

Educators in both the university and the public schools are well positioned to contribute in this way. By virtue of our high levels of formal education, we have access to forms of literacy that we can use to influence policy and decision-making. We know how to state an argument, to support it with evidence, and to use language both persuasively and poetically. We bring an informed perspective to discussions about schooling. In the current debate, the voices of everyone but professional educators seem to count. I believe that one of the ways to break into the conversation would be for those in the universities and the public schools to devote our collective skills and talents to articulating the issues in ways that will make sense to our many communities.

Finally, I gather the most hope and encouragement from the classrooms in which teachers are bringing a critical perspective to their work. When I talk and visit with classroom teachers like Linda Cook, Florence MacLean-Kanary, Susan Settle, Jim Albright, and Vivian Vasquez, I not only gain renewed respect for them as professionals but I also feel a stronger sense of responsibility to support them in any way I can. When I read about how contributors to *Rethinking Schools*, a newspaper published by Milwaukee teachers, are confronting issues of equity and social justice in their classrooms, I see what is possible and continue my own work with a new sense of urgency. There is a growing community of these teachers who are educating children and adolescents for democracy. They are still a small minority of our total teaching force, but in them rests my hope for the future. They rekindle some of my early idealism that it is possible to transform schools.

I have long since abandoned naive and romanticized notions about teaching and learning. I know classrooms and schools reflect all the inequities and injustices that pervade in our society. I know bringing about educational change requires more than a powerful theory of learning; it demands a strong sense of the political. I do not underestimate the difficulty of the project that critical whole language educators have before us. In this book I have described the kinds of profound institutional changes that I think need to take place if critical whole language classrooms are to prosper and multiply. I believe we need to take seriously the messages of critical whole language theory and to work to change the contexts in which both teachers and students live, learn, and work. We need to invent new forms of professional development and school and district organization—forms that foster collaboration, equity, and the valuing of diverse perspectives. I know that there are many forces working against the development of democratic schools. I am aware that many of my colleagues in educational administration view my stance as overly philosophical, impractical, and unrealistic given the times within which we live.

Not too long ago, I read a commentary in which the author advances an eloquent argument against those kinds of critics. Titled "Thinking and Doing the Best Things in the

Worst Times" (Marty 1994), the article seems to speak directly to me and others who continue to work for democratic forms of schooling. Marty writes about how individuals and communities have risen above circumstances throughout history: "Every age has its inner contradictions, but we do not allow these contradictions to be readily apparent or perceived. Yet, in the midst of each era, significant people engage in counteractions, produce countersigns" (225). I believe that critical whole language is a counteraction against social practices that disempower teachers and learners, and I am confident that educators working from a critical whole language perspective have the potential not only to reform but to transform education. This book is both a narrative and a critique, but most of all it is my plea to whole language educators to take up that political agenda—to provide a critical alternative both to "back to basics" curricula and to apolitical versions of whole language that perpetuate the status quo. There have certainly been worse times in history in which to live, but I am sure few would describe our present circumstances as good. There is no doubt in my mind that we need to "engage in counteractions" and to "produce countersigns." I have shared my thoughts about how that might be done; it will be up to each one of us to determine if we will be among the significant people who think and do "the best things" in these difficult and challenging times.

References

Adams, H. 1994. *Peace in the Classroom.* Winnipeg, MB: Peguis.

Albright, J. 1995. *Literacy Conflicts: Who Needs Them?* Master's thesis, Mount Saint Vincent University, Halifax, NS.

Atwell, N. 1987. *In the Middle.* Portsmouth, NH: Boynton-Cook.

Barlow, M., and H. Robertson. 1994. *Class Warfare.* Toronto: Key Porter Books.

Barnes, D. 1976. *From Communication to Curriculum.* New York: Penguin Books.

Barth, R. S. 1986. "On Sheep and Goats and School Reform." *Phi Delta Kappan* 68 (4): 293–296.

———. 1991. *Improving Schools From Within.* San Francisco: Jossey-Bass.

Bigelow, B., L. Christenson, S. Karp, B. Miner, and B. Peterson, eds. 1994. *Rethinking Our Classrooms.* Milwaukee: Rethinking Our Schools.

Booth, D., and C. Thornley-Hall, eds. 1991a. *The Talk Curriculum.* Markham, ON: Pembroke.

———, eds. 1991b. *Classroom Talk.* Markham, ON: Pembroke.

Bracey, G. W. 1991. "Why Can't They Be Like We Were?" *Phi Delta Kappan* 73 (2): 104–117.

———. 1992. "The Second Bracey Report on the Condition of Public Education." *Phi Delta Kappan* 74 (2): 104–117.

———. 1993. "The Third Bracey Report on the Condition of Public Education." *Phi Delta Kappan* 75 (2): 104–117.

———. 1994. "The Fourth Bracey Report on the Condition of Public Education." *Phi Delta Kappan* 76 (2): 114–127.

Brown, R. D. 1991. *Schools of Thought.* San Francisco: Jossey-Bass.

Bruner, J. S. 1960. *The Process of Education.* New York: Random House.

Bryk, A. S., J. Q. Easton, D. Kerbow, S. G. Rollow, and P. A. Sebring. 1994. "The State of Chicago School Reform." *Phi Delta Kappan* 76 (1): 74–78.

Calkins, L. M. 1983. *Lessons From a Child*. Portsmouth, NH: Heinemann.

——. 1991. *Living Between the Lines*. Portsmouth, NH: Heinemann.

——. 1995. *The Art of Teaching Writing*. 2d ed. Portsmouth, NH: Heinemann.

Chambers, A. 1985. *Booktalk*. London: The Bodley Head.

——. 1993. *Tell Me*. Newtown, NSW, Australia: Primary English Teaching Association.

Christian-Smith, L., ed. 1993. *Texts of Desire: Essays on Fiction, Femininity and Schooling*. London: The Falmer Press.

Church, S. M. 1984. "Danny: A Case of an Instructionally Induced Reading Problem." In *Whole Language Theory in Use*, ed. J. M. Newman, 169–180. Portsmouth, NH: Heinemann.

——, ed. 1989. *From Teacher to Teacher: Opening Our Doors*. Halifax, NS: Halifax County–Bedford District School Board.

——. 1992. "Rethinking Whole Language: The Politics of Educational Change." In *Becoming Political*, ed. P. Shannon, 238–249. Portsmouth, NH: Heinemann.

——. 1994. "Is Whole Language Really Warm and Fuzzy?" *The Reading Teacher* 47 (5): 362–370.

Church, S. M., J. Portelli, C. MacInnis, A. Vibert, and U. Kelly. 1994. "Reconsidering Whole Language: Five Perspectives." *English Quarterly* 27 (1–2): 5–14.

Comber, B. 1993. "Early Reading at School: Beyond Strategies, Techniques and Methodologies." In *Reading*, ed. J. Rivalland. NSW, Australia: Primary Elementary Teachers Association.

Cook, L. 1992. "Out of the Straitjacket." In *Becoming Political*, ed. P. Shannon, 286–291. Portsmouth, NH: Heinemann.

Cuban, L. 1988. "A Fundamental Puzzle of School Reform." *Phi Delta Kappan* 69 (5): 341–344.

Cunningham, P. M., and J. W. Cunningham. 1992. "Making Words: Enhancing the Invented Spelling-Decoding Connection." *The Reading Teacher* 46 (2): 106–115.

Dewey, J. 1938. *Education and Experience*. New York: Macmillan.

——. 1944. *Democracy and Education*. New York: Macmillan.

Dombey. 1992. *Reading Recovery: A Real Solution to a Real Problem?* Brighton: University of Brighton Literacy Centre.

Dudley-Marling, C. 1994. "The Role of Programs like Reading Recovery in Discouraging Educational Reform." Paper presented at the Annual Conference of the International Reading Association, Toronto, Ontario.

Dunlap, D. M., and P. A. Schmuck, eds. 1995. *Women Leading in Education*. Albany: State University of New York.

Dyson, A. H. 1994. "Confronting the Split Between 'The Child' and Children: Toward New Curricular Visions of the Child Writer." *English Education* 26 (1): 12–28.

Edelsky, C. 1991. *With Literacy and Justice for All*. New York: Falmer.

———. 1994. "Education for Democracy." *Language Arts* 71 (4): 252–257.

Fairclough, N., ed. 1992. *Critical Language Awareness*. Harlow, UK: Longman.

Field, J. C., and D. W. Jardine. 1994. "'Bad Examples' as Interpretive Opportunities: On the Need for Whole Language to Own Its Shadow." *Language Arts* 71 (4): 258–263.

Freire, P., and D. Macedo. 1987. *Literacy—Reading the Word and the World*. New York: Bergin and Garvey.

Fullan, M. G. 1993. *Change Forces*. New York: Falmer.

Fullan, M. G., and A. Hargreaves. 1991. *What's Worth Fighting For? Working Together for Your School*. Toronto: Ontario Public School Teachers' Federation.

Fullan, M. G., and M. Miles. 1992. "Getting Reform Right: What Works and What Doesn't." *Phi Delta Kappan* 73 (10): 745–752.

Fullan, M. G., with S. Stiegelbauer. 1991. *The New Meaning of Educational Change*. New York: Teachers College Press.

Gee, J. P. 1987. "What Is Literacy?" *The Journal of Natural Inquiry* 2 (1): 3–11.

Giroux, H. A. 1987. "Critical Literacy and Student Experience: Donald Graves' Approach to Literacy." *Language Arts* 64 (2): 175–181.

Giroux, H. A., and P. McLaren. 1986. "Teacher Education and the Politics of Engagement: The Case for Democratic Schooling." *Harvard Educational Review* 56 (3): 213–238.

Goodman, K. 1967. "Reading: A Psycholinguistic Guessing Game." *Journal of the Reading Specialist* 6: 126–135.

Goodman, Y. M., D. J. Watson, and C. L. Burke. 1987. *Reading Miscue Inventory*. New York: Richard Owens.

Gosetti, P. P., and E. Rusch. 1995. "Re-examining Educational Leadership: Challenging Assumptions." In *Women Leading in Education*, ed. D. Dunlap and P. A. Schmuck, 11–35. Albany: State University of New York.

Graves, D. H. 1983. *Writing: Teachers and Children at Work*. Portsmouth, NH: Heinemann.

———. 1994. *A Fresh Look at Writing*. Portsmouth, NH: Heinemann.

Grumet, M. 1988. *Bitter Milk*. Amherst, MA: University of Massachusetts Press.

Hansen, J. 1987. *When Writers Read*. Portsmouth, NH: Heinemann.

Hargreaves, A. 1994. *Changing Teachers, Changing Times*. Toronto: OISE.

Harman, S., and C. Edelsky. 1989. "The Risks of Whole Language Literacy: Alienation and Connection." *Language Arts* 66 (4): 392–406.

Harste, J. C., V. A. Woodward, and C. L. Burke. 1984. *Language Stories and Literacy Lessons*. Portsmouth, NH: Heinemann.

Harwayne, S. 1992. *Lasting Impressions*. Portsmouth, NH: Heinemann.

Heilbrun, C. G. 1988. *Writing a Woman's Life*. New York: Ballantine.

Helgeson, S. 1990. *The Female Advantage*. New York: Doubleday.

———. 1995. *The Web of Inclusion*. New York: Doubleday.

Hiebert, E. 1994. "Reading Recovery in the United States: What Difference Does It Make to an Age Cohort?" *Educational Researcher* 23 (9): 15–25.

Holt, J. 1964. *How Children Fail*. New York: Dell.

Language Arts in the Elementary School. 1986. Halifax, NS: Nova Scotia Department of Education.

Lankshear, C. 1994. *Critical Literacy*. Occasional Paper No. 3, Australian Curriculum Studies Association.

Little, J. 1972. *From Anna*. New York: Harper and Row.

Marty, M. E. 1994. "Thinking and Doing the Best Things in the Worst Times." *Journal of Curriculum and Supervision* 9 (3): 225–232.

McLaren, P. 1989. *Life in Schools*. New York: Longman.

Mills, H., T. O'Keefe, and D. Stephens. 1992. *Looking Closely*. Urbana, IL: National Council of Teachers of English.

Murray, D. 1982. *Learning by Teaching*. Portsmouth, NH: Boynton-Cook.

Newman, J. M. 1984a. *The Craft of Children's Writing*. Toronto: Scholastic.

———, ed. 1984b. *Whole Language: Theory in Use*. Portsmouth, NH: Heinemann.

———. 1987. "Learning to Teach by Uncovering Our Assumptions." *Language Arts* 64 (7): 727–737.

———. 1991. *Interwoven Conversations*. Toronto: OISE.

Newman, J. M., and S. M. Church. 1990. "Myths of Whole Language." *The Reading Teacher* 44 (1): 20–26.

Phenix, J. 1995. *Teaching the Skills*. Markham, ON: Pembroke.

Phenix, J., and D. Scott-Dunne. 1991. *Spelling Instruction That Makes Sense*. Markham, ON: Pembroke.

Pierce, K. M., and C. J. Gilles. 1993. *Cycles of Meaning*. Portsmouth, NH: Heinemann.

Pikulski, J. J. 1994. "Preventing Reading Failure: A Review of Five Effective Programs." The *Reading Teacher* 48 (1): 30–39.

Pinnell, G. S., M. D. Fried, and R. M. Eustace. 1991. "Reading Recovery: Learning How to Make a Difference." In *Bridges to Literacy*, ed. D. E. DeFord, C. A. Lyons, and G. S Pinnell, 11–36. Portsmouth, NH: Heinemann.

Portelli, J. P., and S. M. Church. 1995. "Whole Language and Philosophy with Children: A Dialog of Hope." In *Children, Philosophy and Democracy*, ed. J. P. Portelli and R. F. Reed, 75–117. Calgary: Detselig.

Postman, N., and C. Weingartner. 1969. *Teaching as a Subversive Activity*. New York: Dell.

Probst, R. E. 1988. *Response and Analysis*. Portsmouth, NH: Boynton-Cook.

Rhodes, L. K., and C. Dudley-Marling. 1988. *Readers and Writers With a Difference*. Portsmouth, NH: Heinemann.

Riley, M. N. 1992. "If It Looks Like Manure . . ." *Phi Delta Kappan* 74 (3): 239–241.

Rosenblatt, L. 1978. *The Reader, the Text, the Poem*. Carbondale, IL: Southern Illinois University Press.

Routman, R. 1991. *Invitations*. Portsmouth, NH: Heinemann.

Schein, E. H. 1992. *Organizational Culture and Leadership*. 2d ed. San Francisco: Jossey-Bass.

Schlechty, P. C. 1990. *Schools for the 21st Century*. San Francisco: Jossey-Bass.

Scott, R. 1993. *Spelling: Sharing the Secrets*. Toronto: Gage.

Senge, P. M. 1990. *The Fifth Discipline*. New York: Doubleday.

Sergiovanni, T. J. 1992. *Moral Leadership*. San Francisco: Jossey-Bass.

Shannon, P. 1992. *Becoming Political*. Portsmouth, NH: Heinemann.

———. 1993. "Developing Democratic Voices." *The Reading Teacher* 47 (2): 86–94.

Shor, I. 1992. *Empowering Education: Critical Thinking for Social Change*. Chicago: The University of Chicago Press.

Short, K. G. 1991. "Literacy Environments That Support Strategic Readers." In *Bridges to Literacy*, ed. D. E. DeFord, C. A. Lyons, and G. S. Pinnell, 97–118. Portsmouth, NH: Heinemann.

Short, K. G., and K. M. Pierce. 1990. *Talking About Books*. Portsmouth, NH: Heinemann.

Simon, R. I. 1987. "Empowerment as a Pedagogy of Possibility." *Language Arts* 64 (4): 370–382.

Sizer, T. R. 1992. *Horace's School*. Boston: Houghton Mifflin.

Smith, D. E. 1987. *The Everyday World as Problematic*. Toronto: University of Toronto Press.

Smith, F. 1971. *Understanding Reading*. New York: Holt, Rinehart, and Winston.

———. 1978. *Reading Without Nonsense*. New York: Teachers College Press.

———. 1981. "Demonstrations, Engagement and Sensitivity: A Revised Approach to Language Learning." *Language Arts* 58 (1): 103–112.

———. 1982. *Writing and the Writer*. New York: Holt, Rinehart and Winston.

————. 1983. "Reading Like a Writer." *Language Arts* 60 (5): 558–567.

Smyth, J. 1992. "Teachers' Work and the Politics of Reflection." *American Educational Research Journal* 29 (2): 267–300.

"State Standards-Setting Efforts Dogged by Politics." 1995. *The Council Chronicles* (June). Urbana, IL: NCTE.

The Supportive Classroom: Literacy for All. 1988. Halifax, NS: Halifax County–Bedford District School Board.

Tewell, K. J. 1995. "Despair at the Central Office." *Educational Leadership* 52 (7): 65–68.

Tough, J. 1985. *Listening to Children Talking.* London: Ward Lock.

Trimbur, J. 1989. "Consensus and Difference in Collaborative Learning." *College English* 51 (6): 602–616.

Tyack, D. 1993. "School Governance in the United States: Historical Puzzles and Anomalies." In *Decentralization and School Improvement—Can We Fulfill the Promise?*, ed. J. Hannoway and M. Carnoy, 1–32. San Francisco: Jossey-Bass.

Tye, K. A. 1992. "Restructuring Our Schools—Beyond the Rhetoric." *Phi Delta Kappan* 74 (1): 8–14.

Wilde, S. 1992. *You Kan Red This! Spelling and Punctuation for Whole Language Classrooms, K–6.* Portsmouth, NH: Heinemann.

Willinsky, J. 1990. *The New Literacy.* New York: Routledge.

Index